Advance Praise for *The Buddhist Chef*

"Bring your appetite and check any plant-based skepticism at the door! Jean-Philippe Cyr proves himself a creative culinary genius, offering up one mouth-watering recipe after the next in *The Buddhist Chef*. On a mission to make plant-based eating accessible to all, the recipes in this cookbook are approachable, delicious, and will leave you coming back for more! BLTs. Millet pot pie. Spicy peanut tofu. So. Much. Yes! Jean-Philippe proves, one recipe at a time, that vegan cooking requires no sacrifice at all!"
—**CHLOE COSCARELLI,** vegan chef and cookbook author

"Jean-Philippe Cyr masterfully demonstrates that plant-based eating doesn't mean abandoning everything you love. These recipes are easy, delicious, and perfect for any kitchen."
—**STEVE JENKINS** and **DEREK WALTER**, co-founders of the Happily Ever Esther Farm Sanctuary and *New York Times* bestselling authors

"*The Buddhist Chef* is such a delight to read and aspire to—the marriage of Cyr's spiritual practice with his innovative, yet relatable plant-based recipes is exactly what we could all learn and benefit from. All the comfort foods, the satiating hearty meals that a die-hard meat-lover craves, are laid out in simple vegan alternatives with easy-to-find ingredients. Cannot wait to dive into these recipes and maybe even trick the kids with some veggie meatball sauce! From one hardcore veggie lover to another, Bravo!"
—**MANDY WOLFE**, co-founder and head chef of Mandy's restaurants

"Jean-Philippe Cyr's *The Buddhist Chef* is the perfect blend of nutrition and comfort. The recipes are approachable, full of flavor and well suited for both wellness veterans and those simply looking to add a few more greens to their daily diet. This is a book for everyone."
—**ZACH BERMAN**, author of *The Juice Truck*

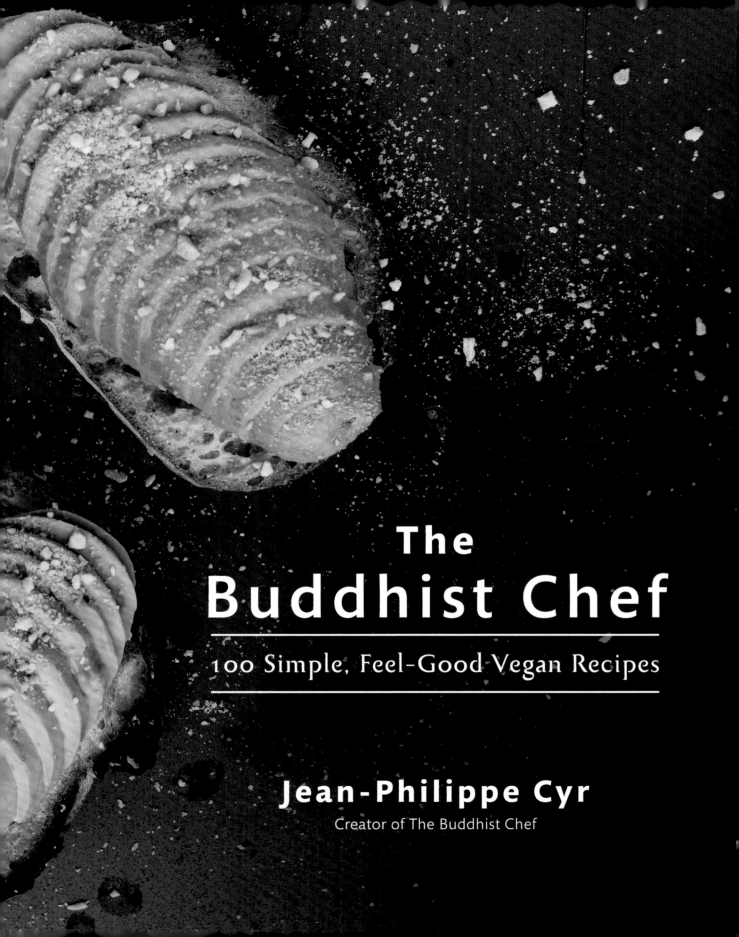

The
Buddhist Chef

100 Simple, Feel-Good Vegan Recipes

Jean-Philippe Cyr

Creator of The Buddhist Chef

Appetite by Random House® and colophon are registered trademarks of Penguin Random House LLC.

Library and Archives Canada Cataloguing in Publication is available upon request.

ISBN: 9780525610243

eBook ISBN: 9780525610250
Cover and book design by Jennifer Lum
Photography by Samuel Joubert

Printed and bound in China

Published in Canada by Appetite by Random House®, a division of Penguin Random House LLC.

www.penguinrandomhouse.ca

10 9 8 7 6 5 4 3 2 1

appetite
by RANDOM HOUSE

Penguin
Random House
Canada

CONTENTS

INTRODUCTION

The tastes, textures, and aromas of food have fascinated me since I was little. As I was growing up, I found myself wanting to experiment with these elements, so I made sure to be in the kitchen as often as I could. Later, I studied culinary arts, and then spent years working in restaurants of all kinds, where I learned how to perfect my skills. I then set off to Asia in search of adventure, new flavors, and cooking techniques.

There, I discovered the Buddhist philosophy and its principles of nonviolence. I briefly toyed with the idea of becoming a monk and never coming back home, but the woman whom I would later marry was waiting for me in Canada.

When I returned, my interest in Buddhism kept growing. I took part in meditation retreats where I would meditate and work as a chef. Since the meditation centers served food that used no animal products, I found these retreats to be the perfect opportunity to learn how to cook with plants and grains and test out new vegan recipes with a focused yet very willing clientele.

As time went on, it became more and more difficult for me to continue cooking with meat as part of my job as a chef. My values had changed, and I was miserable working in a system that promoted principles that contradicted my own. One evening, after cooking lamb for 400 guests at a banquet, I realized I could no longer be a part of an industry that took advantage of the weakest beings. I could not go on like this.

I knew I had to do something—but what? Interest in vegan cooking was growing at the time, which was wonderful news for our health, the environment, and the animals, but many people did not know where to begin. My wife then gave me the idea of gathering all the knowledge I had acquired during my culinary career and using it to promote vegan eating. A blog seemed like the perfect venue because readers from all walks of life would be able to find simple, delicious recipes that use no animal products. And that is how The Buddhist Chef was born!

To this day, I love sharing my recipes with anyone and everyone who wishes to learn how to cook vegan. I try to make veganism accessible and show how simple it is to make a delicious meal using plant-based ingredients you can easily find at your grocery store.

This cookbook, my first, is my way of helping you to cook vegan simply and flavorfully.

It contains my "classic" recipes, the ones my virtual community members appreciate the most. It also features brand-new, fun, and mouthwatering recipes that everyone at your table will love. Whether you are vegan, vegetarian, or simply trying to decrease your meat consumption, I hope you'll enjoy these easy-to-follow and, above all, delicious recipes!

Jean-Philippe Cyr
The Buddhist Chef
October 2018

THE BUDDHIST CHEF
KITCHEN BASICS

Before you begin cooking, here is a list of my tried and true ingredients, as well as equipment, to make your foray into vegan cuisine simple.

Ingredients

Agar-agar is a gelling agent made from algae that is used in tiny quantities to change the texture of food. It's a perfect vegan ingredient to replace animal-based gelatin. To activate agar-agar, you need to dissolve it in a liquid and then bring it to a boil. The magic happens when the mixture cools down. There are two types of agar-agar on the market: powder and flakes. I recommend using powdered agar-agar, but if you use the flake variety, be sure to double the quantity listed in the recipes to get similar results.

Brown short-grain rice is a nutritious, fiber-rich type of whole-grain rice that contains the bran layer and cereal germ without the rice hull coating. It's delicious as a side dish, and I also like to use it to bind veggie burgers. It requires a longer cooking time than white rice, but soaking it beforehand will reduce it.

Coconut oil can complement recipes of all types. For more savory dishes, be sure to use deodorized (or neutral tasting) coconut oil.

Gluten flour is wheat flour with a high protein content. Gluten is what gives bread its elasticity, and gluten flour cannot be substituted with all-purpose or gluten-free flour. Gluten flour is used to make seitan, a vegan meat substitute.

Kala Namak Himalayan black salt is a type of salt with a characteristic sulfurous taste that is reminiscent of hard-boiled eggs. The easiest way to get it is to order it online.

Legumes are edible seeds from fabaceous plants that are harvested from pods, such as lentils and chickpeas. They are becoming increasingly popular in the West, and the Middle East has been using them in traditional dishes, such as in hummus, curry, falafel, soup, salad, and couscous, for a long time. Legumes have many benefits—in terms of nutrition, price, and environment—and because they're an excellent source of vegetable protein, fiber, iron, and vitamins, they are central to a balanced diet. On store shelves, you can find legumes in cans (already cooked) or dried. Use whichever form you prefer. When you first start adding more fiber-rich lentils and beans to your diet, your body might need a bit of time to adjust, but if you push through it, you'll feel so much better.

Liquid smoke is a water-soluble, natural condiment used in very small quantities. As its name suggests, it gives foods a smoky flavor. You can usually find it in grocery stores near the barbecue sauce.

Millet is a very nutritious grain that is cooked like rice. You can use it to replace meat in burgers or pies, for example. It is naturally gluten-free.

Nutritional yeast is a type of inactive yeast used as a condiment in vegan cooking. In addition to being rich in B-complex vitamins, it adds a cheesy flavor. You can find it in stores in flake form. Don't confuse this with baker's yeast or brewer's yeast!

Olive oil is a must-have ingredient, but I use it sparingly because its flavor is more powerful than that of canola or sunflower oil.

Plant milks are milks made from cereals and grains. I like to use soy milk, but you can substitute your favorite plant milk in most of the recipes in this book. Make sure to always use unsweetened varieties.

Quinoa is a high-protein whole-grain rich in iron. It is excellent as a side dish or salad, among other uses. Cook it like rice in one and a half or two times its volume of water. Note that quinoa grains are covered with a slightly bitter coating (called saponin) that must be removed by rinsing the quinoa thoroughly with water before cooking.

Tempeh is a vegetable protein made from whole soybeans, which gives it even more protein and fiber than tofu. Tempeh is fermented and has a more compact texture and a more pronounced flavor than tofu. It's not smooth, either—you can still see and crunch the soybeans. Its taste is somewhat like that of mushrooms, walnuts, or yeast. It has a complex flavor full of umami, the famous fifth fundamental taste (in addition to sweet, sour, salty, and bitter). Tempeh comes from Indonesia, where it is a staple used in many ways (fresh or dried, for example). It is very high in antioxidants and isoflavones and contains various B vitamins and certain natural antibiotics due to the mold used to ferment it. Tempeh also has lots of fiber, amino acids, high-quality protein, calcium, and essential fatty acids, and it is very low in fat. You can find it in the frozen section of the grocery store.

Textured vegetable protein (TVP) is a dietary protein made from soy flour. When you rehydrate it, it can be a vegan substitute for ground meat.

Tofu is made from soybean milk. Rich in protein and calcium and low in fat, tofu is very versatile and has a fairly neutral taste, which allows it to absorb the flavor of whatever you season it with. For savory dishes, I suggest getting the firmest tofu you can find. The labeling can be confusing, so verify the tofu by touch. Firm or extra-firm tofu should have the texture of mozzarella cheese, for example.

Vegetable oil is a neutral-tasting oil. I like to use canola or sunflower oil.

Equipment

A blender, either a standing or countertop model or a hand blender, is very useful to puree foods—to make soup, for example. Don't confuse this with a food processor.

A food processor is an essential tool that allows you to grind dry ingredients—as opposed to a blender, which requires liquid to thoroughly blend foods. Food processors have interchangeable blades that allow them to cut vegetables in different ways. Choose a food processor that corresponds to your needs; if you mainly cook for yourself, you can likely make do with a smaller 7-cup (1.75 L) food processor, whereas a family of four will need one with a larger capacity. Food processors vary in price according to their motor strength.

Crepes (page 23)

BREAKFAST AND BRUNCH

NO-COOK CHIA OATMEAL

SERVES 1 | PREP TIME: 5 MINUTES | REFRIGERATION TIME: 2 TO 12 HOURS

I have reinvented this very easy and healthy breakfast dish into a simple meal with quick preparation for those mornings when you don't have much time. You can even make this oatmeal in a mason jar to eat on the go or as a snack.

1. In a glass jar or a small bowl, combine the plant milk, oats, and chia seeds.

2. Close the jar or cover the bowl with plastic wrap, then refrigerate for at least 2 hours or overnight.

3. Garnish with maple syrup and your favorite fruits and nuts before serving.

1 cup (250 ml) plant milk

½ cup (40 g) rolled oats

2 tablespoons whole chia seeds

1 tablespoon maple syrup, to garnish

Fresh fruits, to garnish

Nuts, to garnish

Tip: The oatmeal will keep refrigerated for up to 2 days.

SWEET POTATO MUFFINS

MAKES 12 MUFFINS | PREP TIME: 20 MINUTES | COOK TIME: 30 MINUTES

Sweet potatoes have much more in common with carrots than they do with regular potatoes. Their colors are, of course, similar, and they both can be easily sweetened. As they say in Thailand, "Same but different." Sweet potatoes are used in place of carrots in this sensational recipe for muffins that not only make an excellent snack but will make you the star of the next potluck!

1 cup (220 g) packed brown sugar

¾ cup (180 ml) vegetable oil (plus more to grease the muffin cups if not using paper liners)

½ cup (125 ml) applesauce

2 cups (300 g) grated sweet potato

½ cup (125 ml) plant milk

1 teaspoon lemon juice

2 cups (250 g) all-purpose flour

½ cup (71 g) chopped walnuts

1 teaspoon baking powder

1 teaspoon baking soda

1 teaspoon salt

½ teaspoon ground cinnamon

1. Preheat the oven to 375°F (190°C).

2. Line a 12-cup circular or rectangular muffin pan with paper cups, or grease the cups thoroughly.

3. In a large bowl, using a handheld or stand mixer, beat the brown sugar, oil, and applesauce for 2 minutes.

4. Add the grated sweet potato, plant milk, and lemon juice. Stir to combine.

5. In another bowl, whisk together the flour, walnuts, baking powder, baking soda, salt, and cinnamon.

6. Add the dry ingredients to the wet ingredients and stir to combine.

7. Divide the batter between the prepared muffin cups.

8. Bake for about 30 minutes, or until a toothpick inserted in the center of a muffin comes out clean.

9. Remove from the pan, let cool on a wire rack, then enjoy.

Tip: The muffins can be stored in an airtight container in the freezer for up to 3 months.

BANANA BREAD

SERVES 8 TO 10 | PREP TIME: 20 MINUTES | COOK TIME: 45 MINUTES

I really love bananas, but they truly are one of the most temperamental fruits I know—second only to avocados. Bananas always seem to be either unripe or overripe. The day I realized I could actually freeze bananas was the day I finally stopped wasting them. It's so easy! Simply peel your bananas, place them in a zippered bag, and throw them in the freezer. That way you will have perfectly ripe bananas on hand to make this banana bread (one of my favorites)!

1. Preheat the oven to 350°F (175°C).

2. Grease a 5 × 9-inch (13 × 23 cm) loaf pan. Set aside.

3. In a bowl, mash the bananas. Add the brown sugar, oil, plant milk, and lemon juice and beat until fully combined. Set aside.

4. In a second bowl, whisk together the flour, walnuts, flaxseed meal, baking powder, baking soda, and salt.

5. Pour the wet ingredients over the dry ingredients and mix to combine.

6. Pour the batter into the prepared pan. Bake for about 45 minutes, or until a toothpick inserted in the center of the bread comes out clean.

7. Let the bread cool for 15 minutes. Remove from the pan, and let cool completely on a wire rack. Enjoy.

2 ripe bananas

1 cup (220 g) packed brown sugar

½ cup (125 ml) vegetable oil (plus 1 tablespoon to grease the pan)

½ cup (125 ml) plant milk

1 tablespoon lemon juice

2 cups (250 g) all-purpose flour

⅓ cup (45 g) chopped walnuts

3 tablespoons flaxseed meal

1 teaspoon baking powder

1 teaspoon baking soda

1 teaspoon salt

Tip: The banana bread can be stored in an airtight container in the fridge for up to 5 days or in the freezer for up to 3 months.

BREAKFAST BURRITOS

SERVES 4 | PREP TIME: 25 MINUTES | COOK TIME: 15 MINUTES

Eating vegan for breakfast can be tricky. What do you replace eggs with? The best substitute is tofu; trust me. Both ingredients have a very similar texture and taste. In this recipe, I'm using tofu as a filling and pairing it with the classic Mexican dish, frijoles negros. These burritos are a delicious meal you'd have no problem eating three times a day!

FOR THE FRIJOLES NEGROS:

2 tablespoons vegetable oil

1 (19 oz/540 ml) can black beans, rinsed and drained

2 cloves garlic, minced

1 teaspoon dried oregano

1 teaspoon ground cumin

1 teaspoon tomato paste

1 teaspoon maple syrup

⅛ teaspoon cayenne pepper

½ teaspoon salt

½ cup (125 ml) water

FOR THE SCRAMBLED TOFU:

2 tablespoons vegetable oil

1 small onion, minced

½ red bell pepper, diced

4 large white button mushrooms, minced

1 (450 g) block extra-firm tofu, crumbled

¾ cup (180 ml) plant milk

3 tablespoons nutritional yeast

1 teaspoon onion powder

1 teaspoon maple syrup

1 teaspoon salt

½ teaspoon dried basil

¼ teaspoon turmeric

¼ teaspoon paprika

Black pepper, to taste

TO SERVE:

4 tortillas, flavor of your choice

Diced tomato

Sliced avocado

FOR THE FRIJOLES NEGROS:

1. Place the oil in a large skillet over high heat, then add the beans and cook for 2 minutes.

2. Add the garlic, oregano, cumin, tomato paste, maple syrup, cayenne pepper, and salt, and keep cooking over high heat for 2 to 3 minutes, or until the beans start sticking to the bottom of the skillet.

3. Add the water. If your skillet is hot enough, the water should immediately simmer.

4. Keep cooking over high heat for about 2 minutes, or until the liquid is fully absorbed. Set aside.

recipe continues

Breakfast Burritos recipe continued

5. In a separate skillet over medium heat, heat the oil, then add the onions, red bell peppers, and mushrooms. Cook, stirring, for 2 minutes.

6. Add the tofu, plant milk, nutritional yeast, onion powder, maple syrup, salt, basil, turmeric, paprika, and some black pepper.

7. Keep cooking for a few minutes until the liquid is absorbed.

8. Fill each tortilla with frijoles negros, scrambled tofu, tomatoes, and avocado. Fold the bottom of each tortilla over the filling, then roll tightly. Enjoy.

GRANOLA, THREE WAYS

(For each variation)   **MAKES 4 CUPS (500 G)** | **PREP TIME: 15 MINUTES** | **COOK TIME: 15 TO 20 MINUTES**

Nothing makes me lose my equanimity like granola. I simply can't resist this crunchy, slightly sweet snack. I sprinkle it over chia pudding or on my favorite cereal, mix it with trail mix, or just eat it by the handful. Granola is simply the best snack for any time of the day.

PEANUT AND CHOCOLATE GRANOLA

1. Preheat the oven to 350°F (175°C).
2. In a bowl, whisk together the peanut butter, maple syrup, melted coconut oil, and vanilla.
3. Stir in the remaining ingredients.
4. Spread on a baking sheet in an even layer.
5. Bake for 15 to 20 minutes, stirring halfway through.

¼ cup (64 g) natural peanut butter

¼ cup (60 ml) maple syrup

3 tablespoons melted coconut oil

1 teaspoon vanilla extract

2½ cups (200 g) rolled oats

½ cup (57 g) slivered almonds

¼ cup (13 g) unsweetened shredded coconut

¼ cup (21 g) cocoa powder

½ teaspoon fleur de sel

SPICED GRANOLA

1. Preheat the oven to 350°F (175°C).
2. In a bowl, whisk together the maple syrup and melted coconut oil.
3. Stir in the remaining ingredients.
4. Spread on a baking sheet in an even layer.
5. Bake for 15 to 20 minutes, stirring halfway through.

¼ cup (60 ml) maple syrup

3 tablespoons melted coconut oil

2½ cups (200 g) rolled oats

¾ cup (107 g) pumpkin seeds

½ cup (57 g) slivered almonds

2 teaspoons ground cinnamon

½ teaspoon fleur de sel

¼ teaspoon ground nutmeg

¼ teaspoon ground cloves

recipe continues

CRANBERRY AND MATCHA GRANOLA

¼ cup (64 g) tahini

¼ cup (60 ml) maple syrup

3 tablespoons melted coconut oil

2½ cups (200 g) rolled oats

¾ cup (107 g) pumpkin seeds

½ cup (50 g) dried cranberries

¼ cup (28 g) slivered almonds

¼ cup (36 g) flaxseed meal

1 tablespoon powdered matcha tea

½ teaspoon fleur de sel

1. Preheat the oven to 350°F (175°C).

2. In a bowl, whisk together the tahini, maple syrup, and melted coconut oil.

3. Stir in the remaining ingredients.

4. Spread on a baking sheet in an even layer.

5. Bake for 15 to 20 minutes, stirring halfway through.

———————————⟡———————————

Tip: Granola can be stored in an airtight container at room temperature for up to 4 weeks.

———————————⟡———————————

VEGAN SHAKSHUKA

Shakshuka is a dish with a fun name and a sublime flavor that originates from the Middle East. In its classic form, it's a brunch dish that consists of a slowly simmered ratatouille of sorts, topped with eggs. To veganize the dish, I created a rich and creamy veggie egg I'm quite proud of. There's a mysterious ingredient lurking in this recipe: Kala Namak Himalayan black salt, which has a sulfurous aroma reminiscent of hard-boiled eggs. The easiest way to get it is online, but if you can't get your hands on it, don't worry—this recipe will still be delicious.

FOR THE TOMATO SAUCE:

1 (11½ oz/340 ml) jar roasted bell peppers, drained

3 tablespoons olive oil

1 onion, minced

2 cloves garlic, minced

1 (28 oz/796 ml) can diced tomatoes

1 tablespoon cane sugar or granulated sugar

1 teaspoon dried oregano

1 teaspoon dried basil

1 teaspoon salt

¼ teaspoon red pepper flakes

FOR THE PLANT EGG:

2 cups (500 ml) plant milk

9 ounces (250 g) extra-firm tofu

½ cup (85 g) potato starch

¼ cup (15 g) nutritional yeast

3 tablespoons vegetable oil

1½ teaspoons Kala Namak Himalayan black salt (optional)

1 teaspoon onion powder

1 teaspoon turmeric

Salt, to taste

FOR THE TOMATO SAUCE:

1. In a blender or food processor, puree the roasted bell peppers. Set aside.

2. In a large saucepan over medium heat, heat the oil, then add the onions and sweat for 5 minutes.

3. Add the garlic and keep cooking for 2 minutes.

4. Add the remaining ingredients and stir to combine.

5. Bring to a boil, lower the heat, and simmer for 30 minutes, stirring from time to time.

FOR THE PLANT EGG:

6. Place all the ingredients in a blender.

7. Blend to reach a smooth consistency. Add more plant milk, if needed.

8. Refrigerate the mixture to set.

recipe continues

Vegan Shakshuka recipe continued

9. Preheat the oven to 350°F (175°C).

10. Spoon the hot tomato sauce into a baking dish, or into ramekins to create individual portions, making sure to add enough sauce to cover the bottom of the dish(es).

11. Using an ice-cream scoop, create small balls (about ¼ cup/50 g) of the plant egg and drop them into the sauce.

12. Bake for 20 minutes. Serve hot.

CREPES

MAKES 10 CREPES | PREP TIME: 10 MINUTES | COOK TIME: 40 MINUTES

I was trying to concentrate on my breathing while meditating this morning, but my mind kept coming back to crepes. Should I serve them with fruit or just plain maple syrup? Are crepes a breakfast food or a dessert? How many times a week is it acceptable to have crepes? Ah, the hungry mind.

In any case, what's important is that crepes are delicious and easy to make. I like to have crepe batter on hand so I can have a quick, dessert-like breakfast handy at any time.

1. In a bowl, combine the flour, sugar, baking powder, and salt. Add the plant milk, oil, vanilla and whisk until combined.

2. In a skillet over medium heat, heat some oil, then add about ¼ cup (60 ml) of the batter. Tilt the skillet so the batter spreads evenly over the bottom of the skillet.

3. Cook each crepe for about 2 minutes on each side, adding more oil during the cooking process, if necessary. Crepes can be kept warm on a baking tray in a 200°F (93°C) oven.

4. To serve, garnish the crepes with maple syrup and seasonal fruits. Enjoy.

3 cups (375 g) all-purpose flour

2 tablespoons granulated sugar

1 teaspoon baking powder

1 teaspoon salt

3 cups (750 ml) plant milk

¼ cup (60 ml) vegetable oil (plus more for cooking)

½ teaspoon vanilla extract

Maple syrup, to garnish

Seasonal fruits, to garnish

Tip: You can store the crepe batter in an airtight container in the fridge for up to 5 days.

Recipe pictured on page 6.

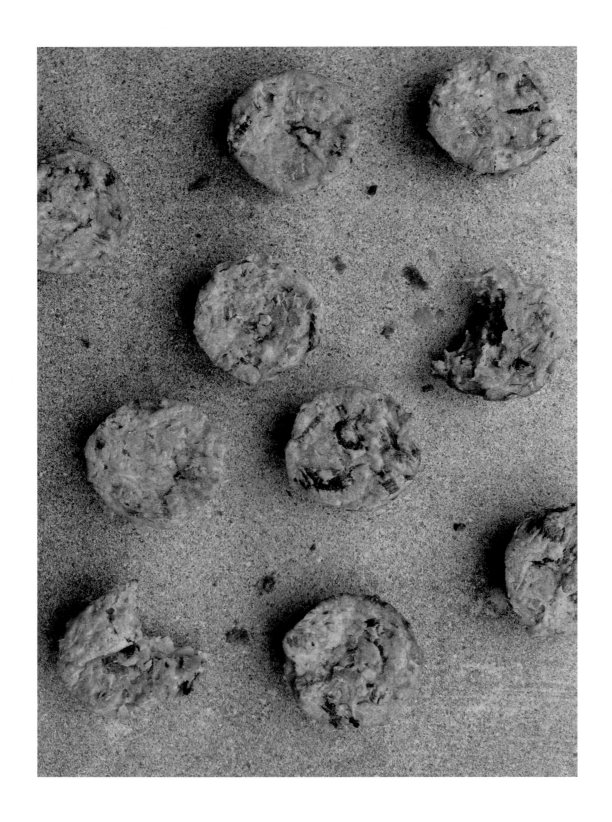

MINI QUICHES

MAKES 24 MINI QUICHES | PREP TIME: 20 MINUTES | COOK TIME: 25 MINUTES

Finger foods are the best! Especially the type you can eat cold once everyone in the house is off to bed. One of the advantages of being in charge of the kitchen in a meditation center is that you can sneak into the kitchen in the middle of the night . . . and grab a snack, just like you would at home. Not that I have ever done that!

1. Preheat the oven to 375°F (190°C).

2. Lightly grease a 24-cup mini-muffin pan.

3. In a skillet over medium heat, heat the oil.

4. Add the mushrooms and leeks, then sweat for 10 minutes.

5. Add the garlic, basil, and oregano, and keep cooking for 2 minutes. Remove from the heat and set aside.

6. In a bowl, combine the chickpea flour, vegetable broth, and nutritional yeast.

7. Add the mushroom and leek mixture to the chickpea flour mixture.

8. Stir well, then season with salt and black pepper.

9. Divide the batter between the cups of the mini-muffin pan. Bake for 10 to 12 minutes.

10. Let the pan cool on a wire rack, then remove the quiches and enjoy.

2 tablespoons vegetable oil (plus 2 tablespoons to grease the muffin cups)

4 cups (227 g) minced white button mushrooms

1½ cups (132 g) minced leeks

1 clove garlic, minced

½ teaspoon dried basil

½ teaspoon dried oregano

1 cup (120 g) chickpea flour

1 cup (250 ml) vegetable broth

¼ cup (15 g) nutritional yeast

Salt and black pepper, to taste

"BLT"

MAKES 2 TO 3 SANDWICHES | PREP TIME: 20 TO 25 MINUTES | COOK TIME: 15 MINUTES

When I first adopted a vegan diet, I had huge bacon cravings. I would literally dream of BLTs! Thinking hard about this sandwich, I realized that as bacon is so salty and smoky, it acts more as a flavorful condiment. But hey, who needs bacon when you can have tofu bacon, right? Yep, I'm saying that you can have your cake (read: bacon)—or in this case, a "BLT"—and eat it too!

FOR THE TOFU BACON:

1. Preheat the oven to 375°F (190°C).

2. In a bowl, combine the soy sauce, maple syrup, oil, nutritional yeast, liquid smoke, and onion powder.

3. Place the tofu slices in a bowl. Pour the marinade over the tofu slices and leave to marinate for 10 to 15 minutes.

4. Grease a baking sheet, then spread the marinated tofu slices on the sheet.

5. Bake for 15 minutes, or until the tofu is crispy.

TO SERVE:

6. Place the tofu bacon, plant mayonnaise, tomato slices, and lettuce on a slice of toasted bread. Top with the other slice of toasted bread, and if you want, you can add a slice in the middle and make it a club. Enjoy!

FOR THE TOFU BACON:

2 tablespoons soy sauce

1½ tablespoons maple syrup

1 tablespoon vegetable oil (plus 2 tablespoons to grease the baking sheet)

1 tablespoon nutritional yeast

1½ teaspoons liquid smoke

1 teaspoon onion powder

1 (350 g) block extra-firm tofu, thinly sliced (see tip)

TO SERVE:

Plant Mayonnaise (page 184)

1 tomato, sliced

Lettuce leaves

2–3 slices of toasted bread of your choice

Tip: Slice the tofu very thinly and oil the baking sheet generously to get the crispiest tofu bacon possible.

BAGELS WITH "SMOKED SALMON" AND FRIED CAPERS

SERVES 4 TO 6 | **PREP TIME: 15 MINUTES** | **COOK TIME: 2 MINUTES** | **REST TIME: 1 HOUR**

People are always astounded when I serve them this "smoked salmon" that tastes similar to the real thing yet is made with carrots. Fried capers beautifully complement the acidity of the lemon juice. You can even prepare vegan salmon one day ahead; it will only taste better!

If you have a juicer and you don't know what to do with the carrot pulp residue, this is the perfect way to use it.

FOR THE VEGAN SALMON:

4 cups (440 g) carrot pulp or finely grated carrots

½ red onion, minced

3 tablespoons capers, chopped

2 tablespoons olive oil

2 tablespoons lemon juice

1 tablespoon liquid smoke

1 tablespoon maple syrup

Salt, to taste

FOR THE FRIED CAPERS:

3 tablespoons capers

¼ cup (60 ml) vegetable oil

TO SERVE:

4–6 bagels, sliced in half

Sliced red onion, to garnish (optional)

FOR THE VEGAN SALMON:

1. In a large bowl, combine all the ingredients, then let rest for 1 hour at room temperature for the flavors to develop.

FOR THE FRIED CAPERS:

2. Rinse the capers, then pat them dry using a paper towel.

3. In a small saucepan over medium heat, heat the oil.

4. Add the capers and fry for 2 minutes.

5. Transfer to a paper towel to drain.

TO SERVE:

6. Spread the vegan salmon mixture on the sliced bagels. Garnish with fried capers and a few red onion slices, if desired. Enjoy.

MAPLE BAKED BEANS

SERVES 6 | PREP TIME: 30 MINUTES | COOK TIME: 3 HOURS, 15 MINUTES | REST TIME: 12 TO 24 HOURS

My grandfather was a lumberjack who spent his winters in the woods, eating almost only beans. Was that the secret to his strength? Perhaps. In any case, this comforting dish would surely have kept him warm during those rough winters.

1. Soak the beans in water at room temperature for 12 to 24 hours. Rinse and drain.

2. Preheat the oven to 325°F (160°C).

3. Transfer the beans to a large saucepan. Cover with water and bring to a boil. Lower the heat and simmer for 15 minutes. Drain thoroughly. Set aside.

4. In a large baking dish or a cast-iron casserole dish over medium heat, heat the oil, then sweat the onions for 5 minutes.

5. Add the molasses, maple syrup, tomato paste, miso paste, dry mustard, salt, and some black pepper. Mix to combine.

6. Add the beans and the 5 cups (1.25 L) water. Bring to a boil, then cover the dish with aluminum foil. Bake for 3 hours, then test for doneness. Add more hot water and keep baking, if needed, until beans are tender. Serve hot.

2 cups (400 g) dry white beans

2 tablespoons vegetable oil

1 onion, thinly sliced

½ cup (125 ml) molasses

¼ cup (60 ml) maple syrup

2 tablespoons tomato paste

2 tablespoons miso paste

1 teaspoon dry mustard

1 teaspoon salt

Black pepper, to taste

5 cups (1.25 L) water

CRETONS

Creton is a terrine traditionally made with pork that you spread on bread for breakfast. It is very popular in Quebec. For an internship I did with an experienced chef, I spent two weeks learning how to make this, along with other terrines and pâtés. I bet he would never have imagined that you could make meatless versions of these spreads that taste even better than the originals! Try this out and let me know what you think.

1 cup (80 g) textured vegetable protein (TVP)

2 cups (500 ml) boiling water

3 tablespoons vegetable oil

4 cups (227 g) minced white button mushrooms

1 onion, minced

1 clove garlic, minced

1 (19 oz/540 ml) can lentils, rinsed and drained

2 cups (500 ml) vegetable broth

2 tablespoons nutritional yeast

1 tablespoon tamari or soy sauce

1 tablespoon maple syrup

1 teaspoon dried basil

1 teaspoon dried oregano

½ teaspoon ground cloves

Salt and black pepper, to taste

1. In a bowl, combine the TVP and boiling water and let rest for 5 minutes to rehydrate. Drain and set aside.

2. In a skillet over medium heat, heat the oil, then add the mushrooms and onions and cook, stirring, for 4 minutes.

3. Add the garlic and the TVP and keep cooking for 4 minutes.

4. Add the remaining ingredients and cook for 15 minutes, or until the liquid is almost fully absorbed.

5. Transfer the mixture to a large bowl, then process using a hand blender until you reach a coarse texture.

6. Let cool, transfer to an airtight container, then refrigerate before serving.

⸺⸺⸺⸺⬥⸺⸺⸺⸺

Tip: Cretons can be stored in an airtight container in the fridge for up to 5 days or in the freezer for up to 3 months.

⸺⸺⸺⸺⬥⸺⸺⸺⸺

TOFU SANDWICH SPREAD

MAKES 4 SANDWICHES | PREP TIME: 10 MINUTES

I'm the kind of person who thinks that any activity is more fun if you remember to make sandwiches ahead of time! A half-hour car ride becomes a fun journey when you have delicious food to snack on. My mom used to make sandwiches using crusty white bread and mayonnaise for any and all occasions. Now I like to prepare my own sandwich fillings one day ahead because it allows the flavors to develop and combine overnight. Hit the road and enjoy!

FOR THE TOFU SPREAD:

1 (350 g) block extra-firm tofu

¼ cup (15 g) nutritional yeast

¼ cup (60 ml) Plant Mayonnaise (page 184)

2 tablespoons olive oil

1 tablespoon maple syrup

1 teaspoon garlic powder

1 teaspoon lemon juice

Salt and black pepper, to taste

2 stalks celery, diced

TO SERVE:

8 slices bread of your choice

Lettuce leaves

FOR THE TOFU SPREAD:

1. In the bowl of a food processor, place all the ingredients except the celery. Pulse until combined.

2. Transfer the tofu spread to a bowl, then mix in the diced celery.

TO SERVE:

3. Spread the tofu filling onto 4 slices of bread, then add the lettuce before topping the sandwiches with the remaining bread. Enjoy.

Spicy Thai Apple Salad (page 46)

SALADS, SOUPS, AND BOWLS

BEETROOT CARPACCIO

SERVES 2 TO 4　|　**PREP TIME: 30 MINUTES**　|　**COOK TIME: 55 MINUTES**

Many people think they don't like beets, but what they actually don't like is pickled beets. Beets are refined, healthy, and beautiful! If there's any recipe that will make you appreciate beets, this is the one. The smoky taste from the chipotle marries beautifully with the slight sweetness of the beetroot. And to top it off, it creates a drop-dead gorgeous (and even photoworthy) plate.

1. Preheat the oven to 375°F (190°C).

2. Spread the slivered almonds on a baking dish, then toast for 3 to 5 minutes until lightly browned. Set aside.

3. Place the red beets in a medium saucepan and the yellow beets in a second saucepan. Cover the beets with cold water. (It's essential to cook the red and yellow beets separately.) Bring the water in both saucepans to a boil, lower the heat, cover, and simmer for 50 minutes.

4. Drain the beets and allow them to cool. Peel the beets under cold running water using your hands or a spoon.

5. In a large bowl, whisk together the oil, cider vinegar, chipotle pepper, and salt.

6. Thinly slice the beets, then add them to the dressing.

7. Refrigerate until ready to serve.

8. To serve, carefully arrange the sliced beets on a serving plate. Garnish with microgreens and toasted slivered almonds.

2 tablespoons slivered almonds, to garnish

2 red beets, trimmed

2 yellow beets, trimmed

2 tablespoons olive oil

2 tablespoons cider vinegar

1 canned chipotle pepper, chopped

Salt, to taste

Microgreens of your choice, to garnish

COLESLAW

I've loved cabbage my whole life. In fact, I love it so much that I think it's written in my biography. Whether it's stuffed with vegetables or used in a soup or salad, cabbage is delicious and versatile. It's also the only vegetable that grows in a handy travel size—just like Brussels sprouts! If you don't know what to make someone for their birthday, just make them this salad—it's always MY favorite birthday dish.

1 small green cabbage (about 1¼ lb/560 g)

½ cup (125 ml) Plant Mayonnaise (page 184)

2 tablespoons cider vinegar

1 tablespoon maple syrup

1 teaspoon salt

1 teaspoon onion powder

2 carrots, grated

1. Slice the cabbage into quarters, then core.

2. In a food processor or using a mandoline, thinly shred the cabbage. Set aside.

3. In a large bowl, whisk together the mayonnaise, vinegar, maple syrup, salt, and onion powder.

4. Add the shredded cabbage and grated carrots and toss to combine.

5. Leave to marinate for 1 hour or refrigerate overnight.

Tip: This is excellent as a side to Millet Burgers (page 83).

POTATO SALAD

SERVES 6 | PREP TIME: 15 MINUTES | COOK TIME: 30 MINUTES

The classic 1970s potato salad is a buffet and family reunion staple. For many (including yours truly), potato salad is a favorite, and inexpensive, guilty pleasure—though its name has redeeming qualities. It's still a "salad," right?

If you make this vegan version ahead of time, it will taste even better. Just don't leave it sitting in your car for too long!

1. Place the potatoes in a large pot and cover with water.

2. Bring to a boil, then simmer for about 30 minutes, or until the potatoes are tender. (Do not overcook.)

3. Drain and leave to cool.

4. Once the potatoes are cool, peel and dice them.

5. In a large serving bowl, combine the celery, plant mayonnaise, horseradish, onion powder, and salt (if using). Add the diced potatoes. Toss gently to combine. Top with microgreens, if desired. Serve immediately.

1 pound (450 g) yellow-fleshed potatoes

1 pound (450 g) blue potatoes

2 stalks celery, diced

⅔ cup (160 ml) Plant Mayonnaise (page 184)

1 tablespoon prepared horseradish

1 teaspoon onion powder

1 teaspoon salt or Kala Namak Himalayan black salt (optional)

Microgreens (optional)

CAESAR SALAD

SERVES 2 | PREP TIME: 15 MINUTES | COOK TIME: 10 TO 15 MINUTES

When I was a child, I once ate at a very fancy restaurant where the waiters prepared Caesar salad right at the table. I wonder if this restaurant is still around . . . or if they continued to allow children at the table after our visit. Anyway, here's my version of the classic salad, featuring coconut bacon.

FOR THE COCONUT BACON:

2 tablespoons soy sauce

2 tablespoons nutritional yeast

1½ tablespoons liquid smoke

1½ tablespoons maple syrup

1 tablespoon vegetable oil

1 cup (50 g) coconut flakes

FOR THE CROUTONS:

3 tablespoons olive oil

⅓ baguette, cut into 1-inch (2.5 cm) cubes

FOR THE DRESSING:

2 cloves garlic, minced

3 tablespoons capers

3 tablespoons Dijon mustard

2 tablespoons maple syrup

1 tablespoon vegan Worcestershire sauce

1 teaspoon tabasco

1 teaspoon lemon juice

½ cup (125 ml) olive oil

¼ cup (60 ml) canola oil

Salt and black pepper, to taste

TO SERVE:

1 head Romaine lettuce, torn into pieces

FOR THE COCONUT BACON:

1. Preheat the oven to 375°F (190°C).

2. In a bowl, combine the soy sauce, nutritional yeast, liquid smoke, maple syrup, and oil.

3. Add the coconut flakes and stir to combine.

4. Spread on a baking sheet and bake for 10 to 15 minutes, flipping from time to time. Set aside.

FOR THE CROUTONS:

5. In a skillet over medium heat, heat the olive oil, then add the bread cubes and sauté until golden brown. Set aside.

FOR THE DRESSING:

6. In a measuring cup, combine the garlic, capers, Dijon mustard, maple syrup, Worcestershire sauce, tabasco, and lemon juice.

7. Blending continuously using a hand blender, drizzle in the oils until the dressing emulsifies. Stop blending as soon as the dressing thickens. Season with salt and black pepper.

TO SERVE:

8. Pour the dressing into a large serving bowl. Add the lettuce, then gently toss to combine. Garnish with coconut bacon and croutons. Serve immediately.

SPICY THAI APPLE SALAD

SERVES 2 | PREP TIME: 10 MINUTES | REST TIME: 30 MINUTES

Inspired by the popular green papaya salad I tasted in Southeast Asia, this spicy-sweet-sour salad is even better when it's made with local fruits, such as apples. This salad is a guaranteed hit at your next picnic! Simple, casual, and slightly spicy—exactly my kind of food.

2 large apples, minced or sliced

2 tablespoons maple syrup

Juice from 1 lime

1 bunch fresh coriander, chopped

2 green onions, thinly sliced

1 Thai chili, seeded and minced

Salt, to taste

1. In a large bowl, combine all the ingredients, then let rest for 30 minutes before serving.

ROASTED FALL VEGETABLE SOUP

SERVES 4 | PREP TIME: 20 MINUTES | COOK TIME: 45 MINUTES

When fall comes around, most of us start craving comfort foods and hovering over a warm stove in the kitchen. This recipe is perfect for the change of season—even the color is reminiscent of the fall! I like roasting the vegetables first, which lends a slight caramelized taste to the dish. I also like to flavor my soups with sweet spices such as cinnamon and nutmeg.

1. Preheat the oven to 350°F (175°C).

2. Coarsely chop the vegetables, then transfer to a large bowl.

3. Add the oil, cinnamon, cumin, turmeric, nutmeg, salt, and black pepper, then toss to combine.

4. Spread the vegetables on a baking sheet or place them in a large baking dish. Roast for 30 minutes.

5. Transfer the vegetables to a large pot. Add the vegetable broth and bring to a boil. Cover and simmer for 15 minutes, or until the vegetables are very tender.

6. Blend until smooth using a hand blender or a stand blender. Garnish with croutons and enjoy.

1 sweet potato, peeled

1 onion, peeled

3 carrots, peeled

2 tablespoons olive oil

¼ teaspoon ground cinnamon

¼ teaspoon ground cumin

¼ teaspoon turmeric

⅛ teaspoon ground nutmeg

Salt and black pepper, to taste

4 cups (1 L) vegetable broth

Croutons (page 44), to garnish

HEARTY MOROCCAN SOUP

SERVES 8 TO 10 | PREP TIME: 30 MINUTES | COOK TIME: 1 HOUR, 10 MINUTES

This is hands down my favorite soup. It reminds me of a Moroccan tajine, a savory stew made with vegetables and spices. The name "tajine" comes from the particular type of roasting dish in which Moroccan stews are cooked.

There's no need to buy any special equipment to make this recipe, but you will want to hunt down harissa, a North African chili paste you can find in most grocery stores nowadays. Be careful, though—it's hot!

3 tablespoons vegetable oil

1 onion, diced

1 teaspoon mustard seeds

1 teaspoon celery seeds

1 teaspoon ground cumin

1 teaspoon ground coriander

1 teaspoon dried oregano

½ teaspoon turmeric

1 clove garlic, minced

8 cups (2 L) vegetable broth

1 (28 oz/796 ml) can diced tomatoes

1 (19 oz/540 ml) can green lentils, rinsed and drained

2 yellow-fleshed potatoes, peeled and diced

2 carrots, diced

1 tablespoon harissa paste

3 bay leaves

Salt and black pepper, to taste

1. In a large pot over medium heat, heat the oil, then add the onions and sweat for 4 minutes.

2. Add the mustard seeds, celery seeds, cumin, coriander, oregano, turmeric, and garlic, and keep cooking for 2 minutes.

3. Add the remaining ingredients and bring to a boil. Lower the heat, cover, and simmer for 1 hour, stirring from time to time. Remove the bay leaves. Serve hot.

MISO SOUP

SERVES 6 | PREP TIME: 15 MINUTES | COOK TIME: 50 MINUTES

Miso soup is one of the essential elements of a traditional Japanese meal. The main ingredient, miso, is a salty paste of fermented soybeans that you can find in most supermarkets. To create a heartier soup, you can add rice noodles. I like to add miso at the beginning of the cooking time, but to maximize its health benefits, you should add it at the end and avoid boiling it.

1. In a large pot over medium-high heat, heat the oil, then add the onions and sweat for 5 minutes.

2. Add the vegetable broth, tofu, miso, mushrooms, and nori.

3. Bring to a boil, lower the heat, and simmer for 45 minutes. In the final 5 minutes, stir in the vermicelli (if using) and simmer until noodles are cooked through.

4. Garnish with coriander leaves and minced Thai chili, if desired.

3 tablespoons vegetable oil

3 onions, minced

8 cups (2 L) vegetable broth

6 ounces (170 g) extra-firm tofu, diced

6 tablespoons (90 ml) miso paste

1 portobello mushroom or 10 white button mushrooms, thinly sliced

1 sheet nori, thinly sliced

Vermicelli (optional)

Fresh coriander leaves, to garnish

1 Thai chili, minced, to garnish (optional)

DRAGON BOWL

MAKES 2 BOWLS | PREP TIME: 20 MINUTES | COOK TIME: 15 MINUTES

Have you ever met someone where it wasn't love at first sight, but then, years later, you ended up marrying them? Well, try tempeh for a similar experience—at first taste, you may not be sold on the ingredient, but then you may very well end up craving it! Made with fermented soybeans, tempeh may remind you of old cheese . . . but in a good way. Let's just say you'll love it, especially in this recipe!

FOR THE TEMPEH:

½ cup (125 ml) vegetable broth

1 tablespoon toasted sesame oil

1 tablespoon agave syrup or maple syrup

1½ teaspoons soy sauce

½ package (4¼ oz/120 g) tempeh

FOR THE SAUCE:

2 tablespoons nutritional yeast

1½ tablespoons vegetable oil

1 tablespoon soy sauce

1½ teaspoons maple syrup

½ teaspoon garlic powder

FOR THE BOWLS:

1 cup (160 g) cooked brown rice (page 57)

Shredded red cabbage, to taste

Sliced red bell peppers, to taste

Grated sweet potato, to taste

Microgreens, to garnish

FOR THE TEMPEH:

1. In a bowl, whisk together the vegetable broth, toasted sesame oil, agave syrup, and soy sauce.

2. Slice the tempeh into triangles and place in a saucepan. Pour the liquid ingredients over the tempeh. Simmer for about 15 minutes, or until the broth is fully absorbed. Set aside.

FOR THE SAUCE:

3. In a bowl, whisk together the nutritional yeast, oil, soy sauce, maple syrup, and garlic powder. Drizzle in a bit of water to loosen the dressing, if needed.

TO SERVE:

4. Divide the brown rice between 2 serving bowls. Add some shredded red cabbage, sliced red bell peppers, and grated sweet potato. Add the tempeh, then drizzle with the sauce or serve the sauce on the side. Garnish with microgreens and enjoy.

MEXICAN BOWL

Mexican food is bold, hot, and tangy, and one of the more vegan-friendly cuisines in the world. This recipe brings all of these flavors together in one bowl. I love it!

FOR THE BROWN RICE:

1 cup (185 g) short-grain brown rice

2 cups (500 ml) vegetable broth or water

FOR THE TEMPEH CHORIZO:

1 (8½ oz/240 g) package tempeh

¼ cup (60 ml) vegetable oil

2 cloves garlic, minced

½ cup (125 ml) vegetable broth

2 tablespoons ketchup

2 teaspoons maple syrup

1 teaspoon chili powder

Salt, to taste

FOR THE BRUSCHETTA:

1 large tomato, diced

½ jalapeño pepper, seeded and minced

1 red onion, minced

1 avocado, peeled, pitted, and diced

Juice from 1 lime

1 tablespoon olive oil

Fleur de sel and black pepper, to taste

FOR THE GUACAMOLE:

2–3 ripe avocados

½ red onion, minced

1 tomato, diced

1 small jalapeño pepper, minced

½ cup (30 g) chopped fresh coriander

Juice from 1 lime

Salt, to taste

FOR THE CHIPOTLE SAUCE:

¼ cup (60 ml) Plant Mayonnaise (page 184)

1 canned chipotle pepper, chopped

½ teaspoon maple syrup

½ teaspoon lemon juice

Pinch of salt

TO SERVE:

Cooked corn kernels

Fresh coriander leaves

Lime wedges

FOR THE BROWN RICE:

1. In a large saucepan, combine the rice and vegetable broth. Bring to a boil, then lower the heat, cover, and simmer for 20 to 30 minutes, or until the liquid is fully absorbed.

2. Remove the pot from the heat and let the rice rest, covered, for 20 minutes.

FOR THE TEMPEH CHORIZO:

3. In a food processor, pulse the tempeh until you reach a texture of rice grains. (Do not overprocess.)

4. In a large skillet over medium heat, heat the oil, then add the garlic and cook for 1 minute. Add the ground tempeh and the remaining ingredients, and cook over medium heat until the liquid is fully absorbed.

5. Cook for a few minutes more to brown the tempeh. Set aside.

recipe continues

Mexican Bowl recipe continued

FOR THE BRUSCHETTA:

6. In a large bowl, combine all the ingredients, then set aside to rest for 15 minutes before using.

FOR THE GUACAMOLE:

7. Peel and pit the avocados.

8. Place the avocado flesh in a bowl, then mash it using a fork.

9. Add the remaining ingredients and mix to combine. Set aside.

FOR THE CHIPOTLE SAUCE:

10. In a bowl, combine all the ingredients. Set aside.

TO SERVE:

11. Place 1 serving of brown rice in each serving bowl, then top with a scoop of tempeh chorizo.

12. Garnish with guacamole, bruschetta, corn, coriander leaves, and lime wedges, then drizzle with chipotle sauce. Serve immediately.

BUDDHA BOWL

MAKES 1 BOWL | PREP TIME: 20 MINUTES | COOK TIME: 30 MINUTES

I love bowl recipes: they're generous and colorful, and they let us get creative. Layer grains or cereals, vegetables, legumes, and dressing, and voilà! That's all there is to it.

Did you know that pumpkin seeds are an incredible source of protein? Speaking of protein, tahini contains more protein than milk. Make sure to keep this tahini dressing recipe close, because you will want to use it in everything. Believe me, it's amazing!

FOR THE BOWL:

1. Preheat the oven to 350°F (175°C).

2. Place the sweet potato and figs in a baking dish. Drizzle with oil, then season with salt and bake for 30 minutes.

FOR THE DRESSING:

3. Place the ginger, garlic, and salt in a mortar (which is preferred) or blender, then mash the ingredients together.

4. Transfer to a bowl and add the tahini, soy sauce, lemon juice, maple syrup, and oil. Stir to combine.

TO SERVE:

5. Place the sweet potatoes and figs in a large serving bowl. Add the quinoa and edamame. Drizzle with the dressing. Garnish with pumpkin seeds and microgreens. Serve immediately.

Tip: If you can't digest raw garlic, don't use it, or cook it before adding it to the dressing.

FOR THE BOWL:

1 sweet potato, peeled and diced

2 dried figs, sliced

2 tablespoons vegetable oil

Salt, to taste

1½ cups (375 ml) cooked quinoa

¼ cup (35 g) frozen shelled edamame, cooked

FOR THE DRESSING:

1 (¾-inch/2 cm) piece fresh ginger, minced

1 clove garlic, minced

Pinch of salt

2 tablespoons tahini

1 tablespoon soy sauce

1 tablespoon lemon juice

1 tablespoon maple syrup

1 tablespoon vegetable oil

TO SERVE:

Pumpkin seeds, to garnish

Microgreens, to garnish

TEMPEH SESAME POKE BOWL

MAKES 2 BOWLS | PREP TIME: 30 MINUTES | COOK TIME: 15 TO 20 MINUTES

Beautiful, healthy, and delicious. I'm speaking, of course, of one of my favorite meals: poke. This Hawaiian dish is traditionally made with fish, and its seasonings are heavily influenced by Japanese and other Asian cuisines. It's simply divine! I make it with sesame tempeh and sushi rice seasoned with my personal touch, which is maple syrup, of course. This beach food can now be enjoyed right in your kitchen.

FOR THE RICE:

1 cup (225 g) sushi rice

1½ cups (375 ml) water

½ teaspoon salt

1 tablespoon rice vinegar

1 tablespoon maple syrup, granulated sugar, or agave syrup

FOR THE TEMPEH:

1 (8½ oz/240 g) package tempeh, diced

½ cup (125 ml) vegetable broth

2 tablespoons sesame oil

2 tablespoons soy sauce

3 tablespoons maple syrup

1–2 tablespoon sesame seeds

1 green onion, minced, to garnish

FOR THE RICE:

1. Rinse the rice under cold running water. Transfer to a saucepan. Add the water, then bring to a boil. Stir, cover, lower the heat to the minimum, and simmer for 15 to 20 minutes, until the water is fully absorbed. Remove from the heat and let rest, covered, for 15 minutes.

2. Stir the salt, rice vinegar, and maple syrup into the rice. Set aside.

FOR THE TEMPEH:

3. Place all the ingredients except the green onion in a saucepan.

4. Bring to a boil, lower the heat, and simmer until the liquid is fully absorbed, about 10 minutes.

5. Serve over sushi rice, garnished with green onion.

Tip: You can also use a mix of black and white sesame seeds for added depth.

"Meaty Burger" Patties (page 86)

LUNCH AND DINNER

VEGGIE MEATBALL SAUCE

SERVES 8 | PREP TIME: 30 MINUTES | COOK TIME: 45 TO 60 MINUTES

Every culture has its own version of meatballs. The Italians have polpetti, the Lebanese have kibbeh, and the Swedish are known for their famous meatballs too. Long ago, I came up with my own vegan version of meatballs, using gluten flour to get that sought-after meaty texture. Forming very small meatballs is the secret here, because they will puff up as they cook.

1. In a bowl, combine the TVP and boiling water and let rest for 5 minutes to rehydrate. Drain and set aside.

2. In a skillet over medium heat, heat the oil, then add the onions, mushrooms and carrots and cook, stirring, for 10 minutes. Add the garlic and keep cooking for 2 minutes.

3. Transfer the mixture to the bowl of a food processor.

4. Drain the TVP and add to the bowl of the food processor.

5. Add the nutritional yeast, parsley, soy sauce, and salt. Process for 1 minute.

6. Transfer the mixture to a large bowl, then add the gluten flour.

7. Knead for 2 minutes, or until the flour is fully incorporated.

8. Shape the mixture into small meatballs.

9. Heat the tomato sauce in a large pan, then add the meatballs and cook for 30 to 45 minutes, flipping them halfway through if they are not fully covered by the sauce. Avoid resizing the meatballs during the cooking process.

10. Serve over pasta.

1 cup (80 g) textured vegetable protein (TVP)

2 cups (500 ml) boiling water

2 tablespoons olive oil

1 onion, minced

4 cups (227 g) coarsely chopped white button mushrooms

2 carrots, roughly chopped

2 cloves garlic, minced

½ cup (30 g) nutritional yeast

¼ cup (15 g) chopped fresh flat-leaf parsley

3 tablespoons soy sauce

½ teaspoon salt

2 cups (260 g) gluten flour

6 cups (1.5 L) tomato sauce (double batch of the recipe on page 68)

Pasta of your choice, to serve

EGGPLANT PARMIGIANA

SERVES 2 TO 4 | PREP TIME: 25 MINUTES | COOK TIME: 40 TO 60 MINUTES

Eggplant is proof that nature has such whimsy: Why else would there exist such a beautifully colorful and fun vegetable? Many people are at a loss when it comes to preparing eggplant, however. How on earth do you cook a funny-looking vegetable that's a member of the tomato family but has a texture similar to a mushroom? Well, here's a simple and delicious recipe that will help you fall in love with eggplant.

FOR THE TOMATO SAUCE:

3 tablespoons olive oil

1 onion, minced

1 carrot, diced

2 cloves garlic, minced

2 (28 oz/796 ml) cans diced tomatoes

2 tablespoons tomato paste

2 tablespoons cane sugar or granulated sugar

1 tablespoon dried basil

1 tablespoon dried oregano

1 teaspoon salt

3 bay leaves

¼ teaspoon red pepper flakes

FOR THE EGGPLANT:

¼ cup (60 ml) vegetable oil

1 large eggplant

Salt

½ cup (64 g) cornstarch

Water

1 cup (108 g) breadcrumbs

1 teaspoon dried oregano

FOR THE TOMATO SAUCE:

1. In a large skillet over medium heat, heat the oil. Add the onions and carrots and sweat for 10 to 15 minutes, until the vegetables are tender but not browned.

2. Add the garlic and keep cooking for 1 minute.

3. Add the remaining ingredients and stir to combine. Bring to a boil, lower the heat, and simmer for 30 to 45 minutes. Remove the bay leaves. Keep warm.

FOR THE EGGPLANT:

4. While the tomato sauce is simmering, preheat the oven to 375°F (190°C).

5. Generously grease a baking sheet with the oil.

6. Slice the eggplant lengthwise (the slices should be about ¾ inch/2 cm thick).

7. Salt the eggplant slices on both sides and let rest for 5 minutes.

8. Prepare 3 shallow bowls: add the cornstarch to the first bowl, water to the second bowl, and breadcrumbs and oregano to the third bowl.

9. Take 1 eggplant slice and dredge it in the cornstarch. Shake off the excess. Quickly dip the eggplant slice in water, then generously coat with the breadcrumb mixture. Set the coated eggplant slice on the oiled baking sheet, flipping once to lightly oil both sides. Repeat to coat all the eggplant slices.

10. Bake the eggplant slices until golden brown, about 20 minutes, flipping the slices halfway through.

11. Serve the eggplant over warm tomato sauce.

EGGPLANT LASAGNA WITH TOFU BOLOGNESE SAUCE

SERVES 6 | **PREP TIME: 40 MINUTES** | **COOK TIME: 2 HOURS, 25 MINUTES TOTAL**

"Why would you ruin a perfectly good lasagna by adding tofu to it?" If that sounds like you or your family or friends, I challenge you to try this recipe! This is the best vegan Bolognese sauce you'll ever have. And the vegan mozzarella cheese has never tasted so good or melted so well. Try it and let me know what you think. Go on now! I'll be right here waiting.

FOR THE TOFU BOLOGNESE SAUCE:

1. Grind the tofu in a food processor. Set aside.

2. In a large pot over medium heat, heat the oil. Add the onions, celery, carrots, and 1 teaspoon salt. Cook for about 15 minutes, until the vegetables are tender.

3. Add the ground tofu, tomatoes, soy sauce, brown sugar, garlic, basil, oregano, red pepper flakes, salt to taste, and black pepper. Cover and simmer for 45 minutes.

4. Uncover and keep cooking for 30 minutes, or until the sauce is rich and thick.

TO ASSEMBLE THE LASAGNA:

5. Preheat the oven to 375°F (190°C).

6. In a large pot of salted boiling water, cook the lasagna noodles according to the package instructions. Rinse the pasta under cold water, drain, and set aside.

7. In a 9 × 13-inch (23 × 33 cm) baking dish, spread a quarter of the sauce. Cover with 1 layer of pasta.

8. Add another quarter of the sauce, and cover with another layer of pasta.

9. Add another quarter of the sauce, then cover with a layer of eggplant slices. Add a layer of pasta. Spread with the remaining sauce, then cover with vegan mozzarella.

10. Bake for about 45 minutes, or until the lasagna is bubbly. Serve hot.

FOR THE TOFU BOLOGNESE SAUCE:

1 (450 g) block extra-firm tofu

3 tablespoons vegetable oil

1 onion, minced

3 stalks celery, diced

2 carrots, diced

1 teaspoon salt, plus more to taste

3 (28 oz/796 ml) cans diced tomatoes

¼ cup (60 ml) soy sauce

¼ cup (55 g) packed brown sugar, cane sugar, or (60 ml) maple syrup

3 cloves garlic, minced

2 tablespoons dried basil

2 tablespoons dried oregano

½ teaspoon red pepper flakes

Black pepper, to taste

FOR THE LASAGNA:

12 lasagna noodles

10 cups (2.5 L) tofu Bolognese sauce

1 eggplant, thinly sliced

Vegan mozzarella (page 81), grated

Tip: If you're short on time, instead of making a lasagna, you can ladle this sauce over your favorite pasta.

WILD MUSHROOM RISOTTO

SERVES 4 | PREP TIME: 30 MINUTES | COOK TIME: 30 MINUTES

This dish is such a classic! I've made hundreds of risottos over the span of my career, and I still love making this Italian staple. It's so simple: gradually add hot broth to rice while stirring constantly. But be advised: you do need to be present and attentive! Think of it as your daily mindfulness practice.

FOR THE RICE:

4 cups (1 L) vegetable broth

3 tablespoons olive oil

1 onion, minced

1½ cups (296 g) arborio rice

1 cup (250 ml) white wine

Salt, to taste

FOR THE MUSHROOMS:

¼ cup (60 ml) olive oil, plus
  more as needed

1½ cups (100 g) whole shiitake
  mushrooms

1½ cups (100 g) whole oyster
  mushrooms

1½ cups (120 g) thinly sliced
  white button mushrooms

½ leek, minced

2 tablespoons maple syrup

½ teaspoon truffle oil

½ teaspoon salt

Fresh parsley leaves, to garnish
  (optional)

FOR THE RICE:

1. In a pot over medium heat, heat the vegetable broth until it simmers, then lower the heat and keep warm.

2. In a separate large pot over medium heat, heat the oil, then add the onions and sweat for 4 minutes. Add the rice and cook for 2 minutes, stirring continuously.

3. Add the white wine and cook for 2 minutes.

4. Add 1 cup (250 ml) hot vegetable broth and cook, stirring continuously, until the broth is fully absorbed.

5. Keep stirring in more vegetable broth, 1 cup (250 ml) at a time, ensuring the broth is fully absorbed before adding more. The risotto should be creamy by the end of the cooking process, about 20 minutes.

6. Season with salt.

FOR THE MUSHROOMS:

7. In a large skillet over high heat, heat the oil, then add the mushrooms and sauté for 4 to 5 minutes, until the mushrooms are golden brown. (Stir the mushrooms as little as possible.) Add more oil, if needed.

8. Add the minced leek and keep cooking for 2 to 3 minutes.

9. Stir in the maple syrup, truffle oil, and salt.

10. To serve, divide the risotto between serving bowls and garnish each portion with some of the sautéed mushrooms and, if desired, some parsley.

MANICOTTI

SERVES 4 | PREP TIME: 30 MINUTES | COOK TIME: 1 HOUR

This recipe is an excellent way to introduce tofu to newbies. In my experience, it's often the slightly rubbery texture of tofu that puts people off, so in this recipe, I eliminated that issue by grinding the tofu. Make these manicotti and serve them without saying a word—the tofu will remain our little secret.

FOR THE TOFU RICOTTA:

1. Add all the ingredients to the bowl of a food processor. Pulse to coarsely grind.

FOR THE MANICOTTI:

2. Cook the manicotti according to the package instructions.

3. Preheat the oven to 375°F (190°C).

4. In a skillet over medium heat, 1½ tablespoons oil, then add the onions and sweat for 4 minutes.

5. Add the baby spinach and keep cooking for 2 minutes.

6. Add the spinach mixture to the tofu ricotta. Stir to combine. Set aside.

7. Cut the eggplant into thick slices (¾ inch/2 cm). Generously season the eggplant slices with salt.

8. In the same skillet over medium heat, heat the remaining 1½ tablespoons oil, then add the eggplant slices and fry for 7 minutes, until softened, flipping halfway through.

9. Lay the eggplant slices flat in the bottom of a baking dish.

10. Transfer the tofu ricotta mixture to a piping bag, then fill the manicotti.

11. Set the filled manicotti over the eggplant slices, then pour the sauce over top.

12. Bake for 45 minutes. Enjoy.

FOR THE TOFU RICOTTA:

1 (350 g) block extra-firm tofu

¼ cup (15 g) nutritional yeast

3 tablespoons olive oil, divided

1 tablespoon maple syrup

1 clove garlic, minced

1 teaspoon lemon juice

1 teaspoon dried basil

1 teaspoon dried oregano

1 teaspoon salt

Black pepper

FOR THE MANICOTTI:

8 manicotti pasta

3 tablespoons olive oil, divided

1 onion, minced

1 (5 oz/142 g) package baby spinach

1 eggplant

Salt

6 cups (1.5 L) tomato sauce (double batch of the recipe on page 68)

MAC 'N' CHEESE

SERVES 4 | PREP TIME: 20 MINUTES | COOK TIME: 15 MINUTES

Some people find it very difficult to give up cheese when they're trying to adopt a vegan diet. In Buddhist terms, this would be called having an "attachment." And what is the opposite of attachment? Letting go. But I have to admit, letting go is much easier if you have a replacement that's even better, which is the case with this mouthwatering mac 'n' cheese! We eat it twice a week at home, no joke. My wife even makes it herself—that's how much she loves it!

FOR THE PASTA:

1 (13¼ oz/375 g) box macaroni pasta

FOR THE SAUCE:

½ cup (71 g) cashews

1½ cups (375 ml) vegetable broth

¼ cup (30 g) tapioca starch

¼ cup (60 ml) deodorized coconut oil or (57 g) vegan butter

¼ cup (15 g) nutritional yeast

1 teaspoon cider vinegar

1 teaspoon onion powder

1 teaspoon garlic powder

1 teaspoon maple syrup

1 teaspoon salt

FOR THE PASTA:

1. Cook the pasta according to the package instructions. Drain and set aside.

FOR THE SAUCE:

2. Pour boiling water over the cashews and soak for 15 minutes. Drain.

3. In a food processor, combine the cashews with all the remaining ingredients.

4. Transfer the mixture to a saucepan and bring to a boil, stirring constantly.

5. Simmer for 1 minute.

6. Add the drained pasta and stir to reheat. Enjoy.

PORTOBELLO BOURGUIGNON

SERVES 2 | **PREP TIME: 30 MINUTES** | **COOK TIME: 50 MINUTES**

This meal is so delicious even mushroom haters will love it. It's because of the red wine, which adds so many dimensions to this dish including a richness and sweetness. Note that once you boil the wine for a few minutes, the alcohol evaporates completely, which means you can serve it to kids and designated drivers.

1. Preheat the oven to 400°F (200°C).

2. In a large ovenproof pot, combine the mushrooms, carrots, onions, oil, cumin, salt, allspice, and black pepper.

3. Roast for 30 minutes.

4. Transfer to the stove, then stir in the red wine. Simmer for 5 minutes over medium-high heat.

5. Add the vegetable broth, soy sauce, tomato paste, maple syrup, and bay leaves. Bring to a boil, lower the heat, and simmer for 15 minutes.

6. In a small bowl, combine the cornstarch with the water.

7. Add the cornstarch mixture to the pot, stirring constantly. Bring back to a boil, then remove from the heat as soon as the sauce has thickened (about 1 minute). Remove the bay leaves.

8. Garnish with parsley and enjoy on its own or with pasta or rice.

3 portobello mushrooms, quartered

2 carrots, sliced into rounds

1 onion, thinly sliced

3 tablespoons vegetable oil

1 teaspoon ground cumin

1 teaspoon salt

¼ teaspoon ground allspice

Black pepper, to taste

1½ cups (375 ml) red wine

2 cups (500 ml) vegetable broth

¼ cup (60 ml) soy sauce

3 tablespoons tomato paste

2 tablespoons maple syrup

3 bay leaves

1 tablespoon cornstarch

3 tablespoons water

Fresh parsley leaves, to garnish

Pasta or rice, to serve (optional)

PIZZA, THREE WAYS

MAKES 3 PIZZAS | **PREP TIME: 1 HOUR** | **COOK TIME: 12 TO 15 MINUTES** |
REST TIME: 45 MINUTES | **REFRIGERATION TIME: 2 HOURS TO 5 DAYS (FOR THE MOZZARELLA)**

As they say, live for today and plan for tomorrow, which is the perfect credo for junk food. Right? Not anymore! This pizza is amazingly delicious *and* guilt-free, thanks to the no-dairy products used. So whether you have a craving or are feeling a little blue, why not treat yourself to a slice of pizza once in a while? With this recipe, you can help yourself to mozzarella, tofu, and veggie-style toppings.

FOR THE VEGAN MOZZARELLA:

1. Soak the cashews in hot water for 15 minutes.

2. Drain and transfer the cashews to a blender. Add the remaining ingredients and blend until creamy.

3. Pour the mixture into a pot, then bring to a boil, stirring constantly. When bubbles start forming around the edges of the pot, cook for 1 to 2 minutes more. (The mixture will be thick at this point.)

4. Divide the mixture between 2 ramekins. Refrigerate for at least 2 hours or for up to 5 days.

5. Remove the mozzarella by gently flipping the ramekins upside down over a plate. Grate and set aside.

FOR THE PIZZA DOUGH:

6. In a bowl, combine the water, yeast, and sugar. Let rest for 5 minutes, or until the mixture is frothy.

7. In a large bowl, combine 3 cups (375 g) of the flour and the salt. Add the yeast mixture and stir well to combine. Cover with a clean, damp kitchen towel. Let the dough rise in a warm, draft-free place for 30 minutes.

8. Transfer the dough to a floured work surface or to the bowl of a stand mixer fitted with the dough hook.

9. Knead the dough for 5 minutes, gradually adding the remaining 1 cup (125 g) flour, until the dough is smooth.

FOR THE VEGAN MOZZARELLA:

¼ cup (36 g) cashews

1½ cups (375 ml) water

⅓ cup (80 ml) deodorized coconut oil

2 tablespoons nutritional yeast

2 tablespoons tapioca starch

1 tablespoon powdered agar-agar

1 teaspoon lemon juice

1 teaspoon maple syrup

1 teaspoon salt

FOR THE PIZZA DOUGH:

2 cups (500 ml) warm water

1 (2¼ tsp/7 g) package active-dry yeast

1 tablespoon granulated sugar

4 cups (500 g) all-purpose flour, divided

1 teaspoon salt

TO ASSEMBLE:

3 cups (750 ml) tomato sauce (page 68)

Sliced mushrooms

Sliced green bell peppers

Tofu Pepperoni (page 187)

Cherry tomatoes, to garnish

Arugula, to garnish

recipe continues

10. Preheat the oven to 450°F (230°C).

11. Divide the dough into 3 portions. On a floured work surface, roll out each portion of dough into a 10-inch (25 cm) round with a thick outer edge.

12. Dust 3 round baking sheets with a generous amount of all-purpose flour. Transfer the rounds of dough to the baking sheets.

13. Thinly spread 1 cup (250 ml) tomato sauce on each round of dough.

14. Garnish the first pizza with mushrooms, green bell peppers, and mozzarella, the second pizza with tofu pepperoni and mozzarella, and the third with mozzarella only.

15. Bake for 12 to 15 minutes, or until the cheese is golden.

16. Right before serving, garnish the mozzarella pizza with cherry tomatoes and arugula.

MILLET BURGERS

SERVES 6 | PREP TIME: 10 MINUTES | COOK TIME: 40 TO 45 MINUTES | REST TIME: 20 MINUTES

I was once challenged by a fellow meditator to recreate the signature burger of a renowned fast-food restaurant whose mascot is a clown. Challenge accepted and mission accomplished! Now you, too, can be a hero and cook this guilt-free version of the popular burger kids love so much. Post a picture of your burger creation on social media and just watch the likes and compliments roll in.

FOR THE MILLET:

1 cup (190 g) raw millet

2 tablespoons olive oil

2 cups (500 ml) vegetable broth or water

FOR THE SAUCE:

½ cup (125 ml) Plant Mayonnaise (page 184)

1 tablespoon minced gherkins

1 tablespoon mustard

1 teaspoon paprika

1 teaspoon onion powder

1 teaspoon maple syrup

1 teaspoon ketchup

1 teaspoon apple cider vinegar (optional)

½ teaspoon celery salt

FOR THE MILLET PATTIES:

2 tablespoons olive oil

1 onion, minced

1½ cups (120 g) thinly sliced white button mushrooms

2½ cups (250 g) cooked millet

1 cup (160 g) cooked brown rice (page 57)

1 cup (108 g) breadcrumbs

¼ cup (60 ml) ketchup

1 teaspoon salt

1 teaspoon garlic powder

TO SERVE:

6–9 hamburger buns

Lettuce leaves

Sliced tomato

Sliced pickles

Thinly sliced onion

Coleslaw (page 40) (optional)

FOR THE MILLET:

1. Thoroughly rinse the millet, then drain.

2. In a large pot over medium heat, heat the oil. Add the millet and cook for 3 to 4 minutes, until lightly toasted.

3. Add the vegetable broth. Bring to a boil, then lower the heat and cover. Simmer for 20 minutes, or until the liquid is fully absorbed. Remove the pot from the heat and let the millet rest, covered, for 20 minutes.

FOR THE SAUCE:

4. In a bowl, whisk all the ingredients together. Set aside.

FOR THE MILLET PATTIES:

5. Preheat the oven to 375°F (190°C).

recipe continues

6. In a skillet over medium heat, heat the oil, then add the onions and mushrooms and cook for 3 to 4 minutes.

7. Transfer the onion and mushroom mixture to the bowl of a food processor. Add the remaining patty ingredients. Pulse for about 1 minute total, or until you reach a coarse texture.

8. Use an ice-cream scoop to divide the mixture into 6 portions, then flatten into patties.

9. Heat an oiled skillet over medium-high heat, then sear the patties for 2 minutes on each side. Transfer the patties to a baking sheet.

10. Bake for 10 minutes.

TO SERVE:

11. Slather the hamburger buns with the sauce, then add the millet patties and garnish with some lettuce, tomatoes, pickles and onions. Add a bun slice if you want to make this a double-decker. Serve with coleslaw (page 40), if desired.

"MEATY BURGER" PATTIES

MAKES 6 PATTIES | PREP TIME: 10 MINUTES | COOK TIME: 20 MINUTES

Sometimes expectations for vegan patties fall flat. They are often soft, bland, and kind of boring. Not this recipe. You can now make a veggie burger resembling the hamburger experience without the meat, and it's not a mushy pâté! It's got a firm, beefy-like texture that can hold its shape. And it's made without the highly processed industrial ingredients. This recipe simply delivers with all the flavor.

2 cups (260 g) gluten flour

¼ cup (15 g) nutritional yeast

½ cup (60 g) chickpea flour

1 tablespoon garlic powder

1 teaspoon celery salt

1 teaspoon salt

1 (14 oz/398 ml) can lentils, rinsed and drained

1 cup (250 ml) boiling water

2 tablespoons tomato paste

2 tablespoons soy sauce

1 tablespoon maple syrup

2 teaspoons liquid smoke

Steak spice (optional)

1. In a bowl, combine the gluten flour, nutritional yeast, chickpea flour, garlic powder, celery salt, and salt. Set aside.

2. In a second bowl, combine the lentils, boiling water, tomato paste, soy sauce, maple syrup, and liquid smoke and blend using an immersion blender until smooth. (You can also place these ingredients in a blender and blend until smooth.)

3. Transfer the wet and dry ingredients to a food processor.

4. Process for about 1 minute or until the dough forms a soft but relatively rubbery ball. Do not overprocess, or it'll result in rubbery patties.

5. Slice the dough into 6 thin cutlets (do not form thick patties) and steam for 10 to 15 minutes, flipping halfway through.

6. When ready to serve, simply put patties on a hot grill or in a well-oiled pan and grill for 2 minutes on each side. You can sprinkle with your favorite steak spice, if you like.

7. Serve with your favorite condiments.

Tip: Once you have steamed the patties, you can store them in the refrigerator for up to 5 days or freeze them for up to 3 months. If cooking from frozen, thaw the patties before proceeding with step 6.

Recipe pictured on page 64.

VEGAN SEITAN STEAK

MAKES 4 TO 6 STEAKS | PREP TIME: 30 MINUTES | COOK TIME: 35 TO 45 MINUTES | REFRIGERATION TIME: 1 HOUR TO 12 HOURS

Summer is right around the corner—well, isn't it always summer somewhere? Which means it's barbecue time! Convert your most stubborn non-vegan guests by serving this seitan steak and delicious caramelized sauce. The liquid smoke, which you can easily find in any grocery store, will enhance that beloved grilling taste. The Kitchen Bouquet seasoning will not only enhance the flavor of the spices but also add a nice color to your vegan steak. Throw in some grilled root vegetables, such as potatoes and carrots, and you've got yourself the perfect summer dinner. Cheers!

FOR THE SEITAN:

1½ cups (375 ml) hot vegetable broth

¼ cup (60 ml) soy sauce

2 tablespoons Kitchen Bouquet seasoning

1 tablespoon maple syrup

1 tablespoon liquid smoke

1 tablespoon Dijon mustard

1 tablespoon miso paste

2½ cups (325 g) gluten flour, plus more as needed

1 cup (140 g) canned lentils, rinsed and drained

⅓ cup (40 g) chickpea flour

1 tablespoon onion powder

1 tablespoon garlic powder

Vegetable oil

Steak spice

FOR THE SAUCE:

2 tablespoons vegetable oil

2 shallots, minced

¼ cup (60 ml) brandy

¾ cup (180 ml) vegetable broth

¾ cup (180 ml) soy cream

1 tablespoon maple syrup

1 tablespoon vegan Worcestershire sauce

1 teaspoon Dijon mustard

1 teaspoon coarsely ground black pepper

Salt, to taste

Fresh chives, to garnish (optional)

FOR THE SEITAN:

1. In a large bowl, whisk together the hot vegetable broth (it's essential that the broth is hot), soy sauce, Kitchen Bouquet seasoning, maple syrup, liquid smoke, Dijon mustard, and miso paste. Set aside.

2. In a food processor, place the gluten flour, lentils, chickpea flour, onion powder, and garlic powder and blend until combined.

3. Add the wet ingredients to the food processor, then blend for 2 to 3 minutes.

4. Transfer the dough to a clean work surface. Knead the dough for 2 to 3 minutes, adding more gluten flour if necessary.

recipe continues

5. Divide the dough into 4 to 6 equal pieces. Shape into "steaks."

6. In a bamboo steamer or food steamer, follow the manufacturers instructions to steam the dough steaks for 15 to 20 minutes.

7. Flip the steaks and steam for another 15 to 20 minutes. Repeat.

8. Refrigerate for at least 1 hour, or overnight, to allow the steaks to firm up.

FOR THE SAUCE:

9. In a saucepan over medium heat, heat the oil, then sauté the shallots for 2 to 3 minutes.

10. Add the brandy and flambé. Alternatively, add the brandy and boil for 2 to 3 minutes for the alcohol to evaporate.

11. Whisk in the vegetable broth, soy cream, maple syrup, Worcestershire sauce, Dijon mustard, and pepper.

12. Simmer the sauce over medium-high heat to thicken. When the sauce has thickened, season with salt if needed.

13. Brush the steaks with oil on both sides, then generously sprinkle with steak spice.

14. Heat the barbecue to high or a grill pan over high heat. Sear the steaks for 2 to 3 minutes on each side—don't overcook, as the steaks are already cooked.

15. Serve the steaks with the sauce. Garnish with chives, if desired.

CAULIFLOWER STEAK

SERVES 2 | **PREP TIME: 20 MINUTES** | **COOK TIME: 20 MINUTES**

Here's an idea: Why not make cauliflower steaks? Grilling cauliflower caramelizes its juices and provides an unexpected depth of flavor. Add a drop of white wine and a pinch of chili pepper, and you've got the perfect side dish, or even a main dish. The secret to this recipe is to use very high heat and avoid moving the cauliflower slices around in the skillet. Patience is a virtue!

1. Preheat the oven to 375°F (190°C).

2. Spread the slivered almonds on a baking sheet or in a baking dish. Toast in the oven for 2 to 3 minutes. Set aside.

3. Slice the cauliflower into 1½-inch (4 cm) slices, then generously salt both sides of each slice.

4. In a large skillet over high heat, heat the oil. When the oil is very hot, add the cauliflower slices. You can also fry these in batches if necessary. Cover to avoid splatter. Cook for 5 minutes without moving the cauliflower.

5. When the slices are well browned, flip and continue cooking for 5 minutes.

6. Meanwhile, in a bowl, combine the parsley, cider vinegar, maple syrup, and red pepper flakes.

7. Transfer the cauliflower slices to a plate. Deglaze the skillet with the white wine and simmer until almost fully evaporated.

8. Add the parsley mixture to the skillet and cook over high heat for a few minutes until tender.

9. Divide the cauliflower steaks between 2 serving plates. Drizzle with the hot dressing, sprinkle with slivered almonds and fleur de sel, and enjoy.

¼ cup (28 g) slivered almonds

1 head cauliflower (2 lb/1 kg) (see tip)

Salt

3 tablespoons vegetable oil

1 small bunch fresh flat-leaf parsley, chopped (25 g)

1 tablespoon cider vinegar

1 tablespoon maple syrup

¼ teaspoon red pepper flakes

⅓ cup (80 ml) white wine

Fleur de sel, to taste

Tip: It's essential to choose a very firm cauliflower head for this recipe.

"SAUSAGES"

MAKES 8 SAUSAGES | PREP TIME: 30 MINUTES | COOK TIME: 1 HOUR, 15 MINUTES

"Sausages? That are vegan?!" Yes, now you can get the taste and texture of the real thing and eat sausages without guilt, thanks to this fail-proof recipe! You'll finally know what's in the sausages you eat, because you're the one who made them.

FOR THE SAUSAGES:

2 tablespoons vegetable oil

1 onion, thinly sliced

1½ cups (375 ml) vegetable broth (plus 4 cups/1 L for cooking)

2 tablespoons liquid smoke

1 teaspoon maple syrup

2 cups (260 g) gluten flour

½ cup (64 g) all-purpose flour

½ cup (30 g) nutritional yeast

1 teaspoon garlic powder

1 teaspoon onion powder

1 teaspoon salt

TO SERVE

8 hot dog buns

Plant mayonnaise (page 184) (optional)

Coleslaw (page 40) (optional)

Tip: The sausages will keep refrigerated for up to 5 days or frozen for up to 2 months.

FOR THE SAUSAGES:

1. In a skillet over medium heat, heat the oil, then add the onions and sauté for 10 minutes, or until lightly caramelized. Transfer to a large container.

2. Add 1½ cups (375 ml) of the vegetable broth, the liquid smoke, and the maple syrup. Use a hand blender to process until smooth.

3. In a large bowl, whisk together the gluten flour, all-purpose flour, nutritional yeast, garlic powder, onion powder, and salt.

4. Add the wet ingredients to the dry ingredients, stir well, then knead for 1 to 2 minutes.

5. Divide the dough into 8 equal portions, then shape each portion into a sausage.

6. Tightly wrap each sausage in plastic wrap or cheesecloth, then tie at both ends.

7. In a large pot, bring the remaining 4 cups (1L) broth to a boil. Add the sausages to the broth and poach over low heat for 1 hour.

8. Remove the sausages from the broth and let cool. Unwrap the sausages, then refrigerate until ready to serve.

TO SERVE:

9. Grill the sausages in a skillet or on the barbecue.

10. Slather buns with mayonnaise or other desired condiments. Serve with coleslaw, if desired.

MOCK CHICKEN

If you have only one chance to convince someone that vegan food can be decadent, this is the recipe you should make. How can you create something so tasty and so close in texture to meat using only grains? With the help of a secret weapon: gluten flour! When you mix liquid into gluten flour and then poach it, it develops a texture like that of meat—so much so that it might actually fool you! This "chicken" burger is the best way to convince anyone to start eating vegan.

FOR THE CUTLETS:

1 cup (130 g) gluten flour

¼ cup (38 g) rice flour

¼ cup (15 g) nutritional yeast

1 teaspoon onion powder

1 teaspoon garlic powder

1 teaspoon dried basil

1 teaspoon dried oregano

¾ teaspoon salt

½ teaspoon poultry seasoning (see tip)

¾ cup (180 ml) warm vegetable broth
  (plus 4 cups/1 L for poaching)

FOR THE BATTER:

½ cup (64 g) all-purpose flour

1 teaspoon garlic powder

1 teaspoon onion powder

½ teaspoon salt

Black pepper, to taste

½ cup (125 ml) plant milk

1 teaspoon maple syrup

1 cup (108 g) breadcrumbs

Vegetable oil, for frying

TO SERVE:

6 hamburger buns

Plant Mayonnaise (page 184)

Lettuce

Sliced tomatoes (optional)

FOR THE CUTLETS:

1. In a large bowl, whisk together the gluten flour, rice flour, nutritional yeast, onion powder, garlic powder, basil, oregano, salt, and poultry seasoning.

2. Add the ¾ cup (180 ml) vegetable broth and stir to combine.

3. Knead the dough for 2 to 3 minutes.

4. Gather the dough into a ball, then slice to create 6 cutlets.

5. In a large pot, bring the remaining 4 cups (1L) broth to a boil.

6. Drop the cutlets into the vegetable broth, then lower the heat to the minimum. Cover and simmer for 1 hour.

7. Remove from the heat and let the cutlets cool in the broth.

recipe continues

Mock Chicken recipe continued

8. In a bowl, whisk together the flour, garlic powder, onion powder, salt, and black pepper.

9. Add the plant milk and maple syrup and stir to combine.

10. Place the breadcrumbs in a bowl.

11. In a deep fryer, add enough oil to cover the cutlets (but do not add the cutlets to the fryer yet), and heat the oil to 325°F (160°C).

12. Dip the cutlets into the batter, then dredge in the breadcrumbs.

13. Carefully drop the cutlets into the hot oil and fry for 4 to 5 minutes, or until they're golden brown.

14. Remove the cutlets from the oil and transfer to a paper towel–lined plate to drain excess oil.

TO SERVE:

15. Serve the cutlets in the buns, garnished with mayonnaise, lettuce, and sliced tomatoes.

Tip: Poultry seasoning is a combination of thyme, sage, and rosemary, to which other herbs and spices are sometimes added. You will find it in the spice aisle of the grocery store.

MILLET POT PIE

MAKES 2 LARGE OR 4 MEDIUM POT PIES | PREP TIME: 45 MINUTES | COOK TIME: 1 HOUR, 15 MINUTES
TOTAL—30 MINUTES (FILLING) PLUS 45 MINUTES (POT PIE) | REFRIGERATION TIME: 30 MINUTES (PIE CRUST)

This is surely one of my most popular recipes. Every week, people write to tell me how surprised their friends and family were upon finding out that this recipe contains no meat. Millet, the star of this dish, has apparently gotten so popular that there are shortages in stores during the holidays. I'm not saying that this is only because of my recipe, but . . .

FOR THE CRUST:

6 cups (750 g) all-purpose flour

1 teaspoon salt

2 cups (454 g) vegan butter, diced

14 tablespoons (210 ml) ice water

2 tablespoons white vinegar

FOR THE FILLING:

1 cup (190 g) raw millet

2 tablespoons plus ¼ cup (60 ml) vegetable oil, divided

2¼ cups (555 ml) vegetable broth, divided

2 onions, minced

4 cups (227 g) minced white button mushrooms

1 cup (120 g) finely diced celery

2 cups (320 g) finely diced potatoes

1 cup (120 g) finely diced carrots

⅓ cup (20 g) nutritional yeast (optional)

3 tablespoons soy sauce

1 tablespoon tomato paste

1 tablespoon maple syrup

1 clove garlic, minced

¼ teaspoon ground cloves

¼ teaspoon ground cinnamon

Salt and black pepper, to taste

½ cup (125 ml) plant milk

½ cup (54 g) breadcrumbs

FOR THE CRUST:

1. In a large bowl, combine the flour and the salt. Using a pastry cutter or 2 knives, incorporate the butter into the flour until you reach a coarse mixture with pea-sized butter chunks.

2. Add the water and vinegar and mix well. (Avoid overworking the dough.)

3. Gather the dough into a ball and wrap in plastic wrap. Refrigerate for at least 30 minutes.

FOR THE FILLING:

4. Thoroughly rinse the millet, then drain.

5. In a large pot over medium heat, heat 2 tablespoons oil, then add the millet and cook for 2 minutes.

6. Add 1½ cups (375 ml) vegetable broth. Bring to a boil, lower the heat, cover, and simmer for 15 minutes. Remove from the heat and let rest, covered, for 10 minutes.

7. In a second pot, over medium-high heat, heat the remaining ¼ cup (60 ml) oil, then add the onions and cook for a few minutes until tender. Add the mushrooms, celery, potatoes, and carrots and keep cooking for 5 minutes, stirring from time to time.

recipe continues

8. Stir in the nutritional yeast (if using), soy sauce, tomato paste, maple syrup, garlic, cloves, cinnamon, the remaining ¾ cup (180 ml) vegetable broth, and the cooked millet. Season with salt and black pepper.

9. Keep cooking for a few minutes.

10. Remove from the heat, then stir in the plant milk and breadcrumbs. Let cool until warm.

TO ASSEMBLE:

11. Preheat the oven to 350°F (175°C).

12. Divide the pie crust into portions according to the number of pot pies you want to make.

13. Roll out 1 portion of dough to a size about twice as large as the pie plate you're using.

14. Gently ease the dough into the pie plate, leaving enough extra dough hanging over the edges of the plate to cover the filling when folded over top. Repeat to prepare the remaining pie plates.

15. Divide the filling between the prepared crusts. Fold the pie crust over the filling to seal the pies.

16. Bake for about 45 minutes, or until the pies are golden brown. Serve hot.

LENTIL SHEPHERD'S PIE

SERVES 6 | PREP TIME: 30 MINUTES | COOK TIME: 1 HOUR, 15 MINUTES TO 1 HOUR, 55 MINUTES

"Everything's better when it's topped with mashed potatoes!" said a wise man who really liked mashed potatoes. But how do you make the best mashed potatoes? When I was working in a French restaurant, we'd just throw in a stick of butter and some heavy cream, which are staple ingredients in French cuisine. But after eliminating dairy products from my diet, I knew I had to come up with a way to keep making delicious mashed potatoes. That's when nutritional yeast—the golden vegan powder—came to mind! The result is simply magical.

FOR THE PUREE:

1. Place the potatoes in a large pot, then cover with cold water.

2. Bring to a boil, lower the heat, cover, and simmer for 30 to 45 minutes.

3. Drain the potatoes, then add the remaining ingredients. Mash and set aside.

FOR THE LENTILS:

4. Preheat the oven to 350°F (175°C).

5. In a large skillet over medium heat, heat the oil. Add the mushrooms, celery, carrots, and onions, and cook for 10 to 15 minutes, or until soft.

6. Add the remaining ingredients and cook for 5 to 10 minutes. Remove the bay leaves.

7. Spread the mixture in a baking dish, then cover with the potato puree.

8. Bake for 30 to 45 minutes. Let rest for 10 minutes. Serve with a green salad.

FOR THE PUREE:

2 pounds (1 kg) potatoes, peeled

¾ cup (180 ml) soy cream

⅓ cup (20 g) nutritional yeast

2 tablespoons olive oil

1½ teaspoons salt

1 teaspoon onion powder

FOR THE LENTILS:

2 tablespoons vegetable oil

10 white button mushrooms, sliced

3 stalks celery, thinly sliced

2 carrots, diced

1 onion, minced

2 cloves garlic, minced

1 (19 oz/540 ml) can green lentils, rinsed and drained

½ cup (125 ml) water

3 tablespoons soy sauce

2 tablespoons maple syrup

1 tablespoon tomato paste

1 tablespoon dried basil

1 tablespoon dried oregano

3 bay leaves

Salt and black pepper, to taste

MUSHROOM POUTINE

SERVES 2 | PREP TIME: 45 MINUTES | COOK TIME: 15 MINUTES | REST TIME: 30 MINUTES

Poutine is a Quebecois dish, which in its classic form is made with three elements: french fries, cheese curds, and brown gravy. This vegan version is just as decadent. I replaced the cheese curds with poached tofu and enhanced it further with the best mushroom sauce you'll ever taste.

FOR THE SAUCE:

3 tablespoons vegan butter

¼ cup (32 g) all-purpose flour

2 cups (500 ml) vegetable broth

2 tablespoons miso paste

4 cups (227 g) minced wild mushrooms

¼ cup (15 g) nutritional yeast

¼ cup (60 ml) vegetable oil

1 onion, minced

2 tablespoons soy sauce

1 tablespoon maple syrup

1 teaspoon onion powder

1 teaspoon vegan Worcestershire sauce

Black pepper, to taste

Truffle oil (optional)

FOR THE TOFU CURDS:

1 (350 g) block extra-firm tofu

3 tablespoons cider vinegar

1 tablespoon lemon juice

1 tablespoon maple syrup

1 teaspoon onion powder

½ teaspoon salt

FOR THE FRIES:

3 large Russet potatoes, peeled

Vegetable oil, for frying

Salt, to taste

Tip: You can finish cooking the fries in the oven if you prefer that to frying them twice in oil.

FOR THE SAUCE:

1. In a large pot over medium heat, melt the butter. Add the flour and continue to cook for about 2 minutes, stirring constantly.

2. Add the vegetable broth. Bring to a boil and continue stirring.

3. Add the remaining ingredients. Continue to simmer for a few more minutes to reduce the sauce.

FOR THE TOFU CURDS:

4. Bring a pot of water to a boil. Crumble the tofu, then add to the boiling water and cook for 2 minutes. Drain and set aside.

5. In a bowl, combine the remaining ingredients to make the marinade.

6. Add the tofu, stir to coat with the marinade, then let rest for 30 minutes. Set aside.

FOR THE FRIES:

7. Slice the potatoes into ¼-inch (6 mm) thick sticks. Add the potato sticks to a bowl of cold water and leave them there until ready to fry, to avoid browning.

8. In a deep fryer, heat the oil (enough to cover the potato sticks once they're added in the next step) to 325°F (160°C).

9. Drain the water from the potato sticks, then pat dry using a clean kitchen towel. Transfer to the fryer basket, then lower into the oil and fry for about 3 minutes.

10. Lift the basket out of the oil and let the fries rest.

11. Increase the heat of the oil to 350°F (175°C).

12. Lower the fries into the oil again and fry for 4 minutes, or until the fries are golden brown. Transfer the fries to paper towels. Season with salt and keep warm.

TO SERVE:

13. Divide the fries between 2 serving plates. Add the tofu curds and ladle with sauce. Enjoy.

MUSHROOM QUINOA

SERVES 2 | **PREP TIME: 30 MINUTES** | **COOK TIME: 20 TO 25 MINUTES**

Quinoa's spelling makes it hard to pronounce, but its nutritional benefits make it hard to fight against! Quinoa is a well-rounded grain that is grown for its edible seeds. It is gluten-free, high in protein, and one of the few plant foods that contain all nine essential amino acids.

Make sure you rinse quinoa well before cooking it. The rinsing process removes quinoa's natural coating, called saponin, which can make it taste bitter or soapy.

1. Place the quinoa and vegetable broth in a large saucepan. Bring to a boil, lower the heat, cover, and simmer for 12 minutes.

2. Remove from the heat and let rest, covered, for 10 minutes. Set aside.

3. In a second saucepan, over medium-high heat, heat the oil, then add the mushrooms and onions and cook for 5 to 10 minutes.

4. Add the cooked quinoa, peas, soy sauce, cider vinegar, maple syrup, and sambal oelek.

5. Season with salt and black pepper and keep cooking for 3 to 4 minutes to reheat. Serve the quinoa garnished with avocado and slivered almonds.

1 cup (170 g) quinoa, thoroughly rinsed

2 cups (500 ml) vegetable broth or water

2 tablespoons olive oil

2½ cups (225 g) thinly sliced wild mushrooms

1 onion, minced

½ cup (80 g) frozen peas

2 tablespoons soy sauce

1 tablespoon cider vinegar

1 tablespoon maple syrup

1 teaspoon sambal oelek or 1 pinch of red pepper flakes

Salt and black pepper, to taste

Sliced avocado, to garnish

Slivered almonds, to garnish

SQUASH CURRY

SERVES 4 | **PREP TIME: 30 MINUTES** | **COOK TIME: 55 MINUTES TO 1 HOUR, 15 MINUTES**

Where Asia meets Europe! Asia is known for its often quick cooking times using very high heat, while Europe prefers slow cooking, often braising foods for a long time in the oven. This recipe combines the best of both worlds: the Asian spices used in the dish develop their full aroma over the long baking time, which also allows the squash and onion to caramelize and develop a sweet, aromatic flavor.

1 butternut squash

2 tablespoons vegetable oil

1 onion, minced

2 teaspoons curry powder

1 teaspoon sambal oelek or
    ¼ teaspoon red pepper flakes

1 teaspoon maple syrup

½ teaspoon mustard seeds

½ teaspoon ground cinnamon

½ teaspoon ground turmeric

½ teaspoon ground cumin

1 cup (250 ml) canned coconut
    milk

1 tomato, diced

1 teaspoon salt

Black pepper, to taste

1. Preheat the oven to 375°F (190°C).

2. Peel the squash, seed it, then cut it into cubes. Transfer the squash cubes to a baking dish. Set aside.

3. In a pot over medium heat, heat the oil, then add the onions and cook until tender.

4. Stir in the curry powder, sambal oelek, maple syrup, mustard seeds, cinnamon, turmeric, and cumin. Keep cooking for 2 minutes.

5. Add the coconut milk, tomatoes, salt, and black pepper, then simmer for 5 minutes.

6. Pour the mixture over the squash.

7. Bake for 45 to 60 minutes, or until the squash is tender and golden brown on top. Enjoy.

ZUCCHINI AND CARROT KOFTAS

SERVES 4 | PREP TIME: 30 MINUTES | COOK TIME: 30 TO 40 MINUTES

I'm not sure why, but people seem to have a fondness for ball-shaped foods—kids, especially. Want your kids to eat more vegetables? Shape them into balls, and voilà! It's like magic. If you're still getting resistance, serve these koftas with ketchup as a last resort, but I'm pretty sure kids will like this recipe's rich and sweet curry sauce even without it.

FOR THE KOFTAS:

1. Preheat the oven to 375°F (190°C).
2. Using a potato masher, coarsely crush the chickpeas. Set aside.
3. In a large pot over medium heat, heat the oil, then add the onions and sweat for 4 minutes, until tender.
4. Add the grated zucchinis and carrots, and keep cooking for 3 to 4 minutes.
5. Add the crushed chickpeas, chickpea flour, water, nutritional yeast, curry powder, salt, and cumin.
6. Stir well, then remove from the heat.
7. Grease a baking sheet.
8. Shape the chickpea mixture into balls the size of golf balls, then set them on the baking sheet.
9. Bake for 20 to 30 minutes.

FOR THE SAUCE:

10. Meanwhile, in a large pot, combine the sauce ingredients and bring to a boil. Simmer for 5 minutes.
11. Serve the koftas ladled with the sauce.

FOR THE KOFTAS:

1 (19 oz/540 ml) can chickpeas, rinsed and drained

2 tablespoons olive oil (plus 2 tablespoons to grease the baking sheet)

1 onion, minced

2 zucchinis, grated

3 carrots, grated

1 cup (120 g) chickpea flour

½ cup (125 ml) water

¼ cup (15 g) nutritional yeast

1 tablespoon curry powder

1 teaspoon salt

1 teaspoon ground cumin

FOR THE SAUCE:

1 (14 oz/398 ml) can coconut milk

¼ cup (15 g) nutritional yeast

1 tablespoon cane sugar or granulated sugar

1 tablespoon curry powder

½ teaspoon salt

¼ teaspoon red pepper flakes

FALAFELS

**MAKES 12 FALAFELS | PREP TIME: 30 MINUTES |
COOK TIME: 25 TO 30 MINUTES | REST TIME: 12 TO 24 HOURS**

Falafels are beloved in the Middle East, and now all over the world. And rightfully so! You can find these balls of fried chickpeas everywhere. They're often served with tahini sauce or hummus. I prefer to bake them, rather than frying, as it makes them lighter and just as flavorful. To get the iconic, slightly crunchy texture of falafel, you must use raw chickpeas, soaked overnight, instead of canned.

1 cup (255 g) dry chickpeas

1 onion, quartered

½ cup (30 g) chopped fresh
flat-leaf parsley

⅓ cup (38 g) slivered almonds

2 cloves garlic, minced

Juice from 1 lemon

1 tablespoon maple syrup

1 teaspoon ground cumin

1 teaspoon salt

1 teaspoon harissa paste (or
1 tablespoon if you'd like a
spicier version)

½ teaspoon baking soda

½ cup (64 g) all-purpose flour

Vegetable oil, for cooking

Coleslaw (page 40), to serve
(optional)

Hummus (page 150), to serve
(optional)

Naan bread, to serve (optional)

1. Soak the chickpeas in water for 12 to 24 hours. Rinse thoroughly and drain. The chickpeas will have doubled in volume, which will provide the necessary 2 cups (500 ml) needed for this recipe.

2. Preheat the oven to 375°F (190°C).

3. In a food processor, pulse the chickpeas until you reach a texture similar to couscous. (Do not overprocess.)

4. Transfer the chickpeas to a large mixing bowl and set aside. To the bowl of the food processor, add the onions, parsley, almonds, garlic, lemon juice, maple syrup, cumin, salt, harissa, and baking soda. Pulse to combine, then add to the chickpeas. Sprinkle with the flour, and mix thoroughly.

5. Shape the mixture into 12 small patties.

6. In a skillet over medium heat, heat some oil, then fry the patties until brown, 2 to 3 minutes on each side. Fry the patties in batches to avoid overcrowding.

7. Transfer the patties to a baking sheet and bake for 5 to 10 minutes.

8. Serve with coleslaw, hummus, and naan bread, if desired.

GYROS

I love Greece. I've traveled there twice, and each time, I came back feeling enchanted by the country. Did you know that Greece is the cradle not only of Western civilization but also of vegetarianism? Many Greek philosophers, including Pythagoras, Socrates, and Plato, recommended a vegetarian diet, and then Roman philosophers followed suit. They did so for ethical reasons. And here I thought my hippie aunt invented the vegetarian diet when I was a kid!

FOR THE "CHICKEN":

1¼ cups (160 g) gluten flour

¼ cup (15 g) nutritional yeast

1 tablespoon onion powder

1 tablespoon garlic powder

½ teaspoon poultry seasoning (see tip, page 96)

1 teaspoon salt

8 ounces (222 g) extra-firm tofu

¾ cup (180 ml) plant milk

1 tablespoon miso paste

1 tablespoon paprika

6 cups (1.5 L) vegetable broth, plus extra as needed

FOR THE TZATZIKI:

1 cup (250 ml) Plant Mayonnaise (page 184)

½ cucumber, finely diced

2 tablespoons minced dill

1 teaspoon onion powder

TO ASSEMBLE:

About 1 pound (450 g) "chicken"

4 large pita breads

Sliced tomatoes, to garnish

Iceberg or Boston lettuce leaves, coarsely chopped, to garnish

Thinly sliced red onion, to garnish (optional)

FOR THE "CHICKEN":

1. In a large bowl, combine the gluten flour, nutritional yeast, onion powder, garlic powder, poultry seasoning, and salt. Set aside.

2. Crumble the tofu into chunks and place in a blender.

3. Add the plant milk and miso paste and blend until smooth.

4. Add the wet ingredients to the dry ingredients and stir to combine. Knead for 2 minutes.

5. Generously sprinkle paprika all over the dough. Wrap the dough with plastic wrap or cheesecloth and tie at both ends.

6. In a large pot, bring the vegetable broth to a boil, then add the wrapped "chicken" dough.

7. Lower the heat and poach the chicken for 1 hour, flipping it from time to time. The dough package should be fully immersed in broth. Add more broth, if needed.

8. Remove from the heat and let the chicken cool in the broth for 15 minutes.

9. Unwrap the chicken and cut into slices or strips.

10. If you'd like to grill the chicken, preheat the oven to 350°F (175°C). Place the chicken on a lightly oiled baking sheet and bake in the oven for 10 minutes, until crunchy.

FOR THE TZATZIKI:

11. In a bowl, combine all the ingredients. Refrigerate until ready to use.

TO SERVE:

12. Lay some chicken over each pita bread. Drizzle with tzatziki, garnish with tomatoes, lettuce, and onions, if desired, then roll and enjoy.

PHYLLO PASTRY MUSHROOMS

MAKES 16 TRIANGLES | PREP TIME: 30 MINUTES | COOK TIME: 30 MINUTES

Have you ever loved a certain food so much that you just don't cook it, because you know you'll eat it all? My weakness is anything wrapped in phyllo pastry. Phyllo is paper-thin pastry commonly used in Greek, Eastern European, and Middle Eastern cuisines for both savory and sweet dishes. Its crunch is so addictive that I sometimes wonder why all foods aren't wrapped in it!

1. Preheat the oven to 375°F (190°C).

2. In a skillet over medium heat, heat the oil.

3. Add the mushrooms and leeks and sweat for 10 minutes.

4. Add the vegetable broth, peas, breadcrumbs, garlic, and truffle oil. Season with salt and black pepper, then keep cooking for 4 minutes. Set aside.

5. Lay a sheet of phyllo pastry on your work surface, then brush it all over with oil. Cover with a second sheet, then brush that too all over with oil.

6. Slice the sheets widthwise into 4 equal strips. Drop 1 heaping tablespoon of filling on one corner of each phyllo pastry strip.

7. Fold the strips diagonally 4 times over the filling to create triangles. Transfer the triangles to a baking sheet.

8. Repeat with the remaining phyllo sheets and filling to create 16 triangles in total.

9. Lightly brush the top of the triangles with oil, then bake for 15 minutes. Let cool slightly before eating.

2 tablespoons vegetable oil (plus 3 tablespoons for brushing)

4 cups (227 g) minced white button mushrooms, minced

1½ cups (132 g) minced leeks

1 cup (250 ml) vegetable broth

1 cup (160 g) frozen peas

¼ cup (27 g) breadcrumbs

1 clove garlic, minced

1 teaspoon truffle oil

Salt and black pepper, to taste

8 sheets phyllo pastry

MOROCCAN-STYLE TOFU

SERVES 4 | PREP TIME: 20 MINUTES | COOK TIME: 40 MINUTES

There is a concept in Buddhism known as "right livelihood," which is a way of living and working that doesn't interfere with your compassionate and nonviolent beliefs. At a certain point in my life, I felt like cooking animals for a living wasn't in concordance with my beliefs, so I quit my job as a chef and began a journey that led me to this book. My goal was to create simple dishes using plant-based ingredients as substitutes for meat. One of the first dishes I created was this Moroccan-inspired tofu dish, which remains one of my favorites to this day.

2 tablespoons vegetable oil

1 onion, thinly sliced

1 (450 g) block extra-firm tofu, diced

8 dried prunes, pitted

1 tablespoon Madras curry powder

1 tablespoon maple syrup

½ teaspoon ground cinnamon

¼ teaspoon ground cloves

¼ teaspoon red pepper flakes

1 (14 oz/398 ml) can coconut milk

2 tablespoons tomato paste

½ teaspoon salt

Black pepper, to taste

Naan bread, to serve

1. Preheat the oven to 350°F (175°C).

2. In a large saucepan over medium-high heat, heat the oil. Add the onions and tofu and sauté for 5 minutes.

3. Stir in the prunes, curry powder, maple syrup, cinnamon, cloves, and red pepper flakes, and keep cooking for 3 minutes.

4. Stir in the coconut milk, tomato paste, and salt, then season with black pepper.

5. Transfer to a baking dish.

6. Bake for 30 minutes, or until the tofu has absorbed half of the sauce. Serve with naan bread.

AVOCADO TARTARE

SERVES 1 | PREP TIME: 15 MINUTES | COOK TIME: 5 MINUTES

Whoever said vegan cooking isn't worthy of the finest restaurants? Your guests will be amazed when they see the refined dishes you can prepare for them. In this recipe, refined doesn't mean complex—I hate culinary snobbery; I believe simplicity always tastes best. Chef's tip: the secret to refined cuisine often lies in the presentation!

1. Preheat the oven to 375°F (190°C).

2. In a bowl, gently combine the avocado, mayonnaise, Tabasco, and a pinch of fleur de sel. Set aside.

3. Using the empty can, cut a round out of the tortilla.

4. Place the tortilla round on a baking sheet.

5. Lightly brush the tortilla with oil, then sprinkle with the oregano and a pinch of fleur de sel.

6. Bake for 5 minutes.

7. Set the empty can on a serving plate. Spoon in the avocado mixture, gently pressing it down and leveling the top with a spoon.

8. Add the toasted tortilla round, then top with the diced tomato. Gently press the tartare down with the back of the spoon.

9. Slowly lift the can. Drizzle with balsamic vinegar and serve.

1 avocado, peeled, pitted, and diced

1 tablespoon Plant Mayonnaise (page 184)

Few drops of Tabasco sauce

Fleur de sel

1 empty (28 oz/796 ml) can, top and bottom removed, for shaping the tartare

1 small corn tortilla

Olive oil, for brushing

¼ teaspoon dried oregano

1 small tomato, diced

Drizzle of balsamic vinegar

CHILI SIN CARNE

SERVES 4 TO 6 | **PREP TIME: 30 MINUTES** | **COOK TIME: 1 HOUR, 10 MINUTES**

Yes, you can use cocoa in savory dishes! Cocoa powder is actually the secret to this recipe and is the basis for mole, a classic Mexican sauce. I was inspired to add it to my Chili Sin Carne recipe, as it truly brings out the flavor of the dish. Serve this chili as a filling for tacos or over rice, or simply pair it with tortilla chips or nachos.

2 tablespoons vegetable oil

1 onion, thinly sliced

2 stalks celery, diced

2 carrots, diced

Salt, to taste

¼ cup (55 g) packed brown sugar

1 tablespoon chili powder

1 tablespoon cocoa powder

2 teaspoons minced garlic

1 teaspoon ground cumin

1 teaspoon ground coriander

½ teaspoon red pepper flakes

Black pepper, to taste

2 (28 oz/796 ml) cans diced tomatoes

1 (19 oz/540 ml) can red kidney beans, rinsed and drained

1 cup (165 g) frozen corn kernels

Fresh coriander leaves, to garnish (optional)

1. In a large pot over medium heat, heat the oil, then add the onions and sweat for 2 minutes. Add the celery and carrots, season with salt, and keep cooking for 5 minutes.

2. Add the brown sugar, chili powder, cocoa powder, garlic, cumin, coriander, and red pepper flakes. Season with more salt, if necessary, and black pepper. Stir to combine and keep cooking, stirring, for 2 minutes.

3. Add the tomatoes, red kidney beans, and corn kernels.

4. Simmer for 1 hour. Garnish with coriander, if desired, then serve hot with rice or as a taco filling.

TACOS

MAKES 16 TACOS | PREP TIME: 20 MINUTES | COOK TIME: 1 HOUR

Did you know that jackfruit can be used as a meat substitute? Yes, it's mind-blowing! You can use jackfruit in lots of recipes, including these tacos, which I guarantee will quickly become one of your favorites. Make sure to use jackfruit packaged in water or brine, not syrup.

FOR THE JACKFRUIT:

1. Preheat the oven to 350°F (175°C).

2. In a large pot over medium heat, heat the oil, then add the onions and sweat for 2 minutes.

3. Drain and seed the jackfruit, then add it to the onions. Cook for 2 minutes.

4. Add the remaining ingredients and bring to a boil. Lower the heat, cover, and simmer for 10 minutes.

5. Transfer to a baking dish. Bake for 45 minutes.

6. Remove the jackfruit mixture from the oven, then shred it using a fork.

TO SERVE:

7. Fill the tortillas with shredded jackfruit, bruschetta, avocado, sliced red onions, Marinated Red Onions, and fresh herbs. Serve with lime wedges.

FOR THE JACKFRUIT:

2 tablespoons vegetable oil

1 onion, thinly sliced

2 (20 oz/570 g) packages jackfruit in brine or water (not in syrup)

1 cup (250 ml) vegetable broth

¼ cup (60 ml) ketchup

3 tablespoons molasses

1 tablespoon chili powder

1 teaspoon onion powder

1 teaspoon cocoa powder

1 teaspoon cider vinegar

1 teaspoon salt

TO SERVE:

16 small tortillas

Mexican bruschetta (page 57)

1 avocado, peeled, pitted, and diced

1 red onion, thinly sliced

Marinated Red Onions (page 185)

Fresh herbs, such as coriander

Lime wedges, to serve

CORN TAMALES

MAKES 6 TO 8 TAMALES | PREP TIME: 30 MINUTES | COOK TIME: 15 MINUTES

Originally, tamales were steamed packets of cornhusks stuffed with a dough made from cornmeal. They were made that way so they could be easily transported. There were as many tamale varieties as there are sandwiches today. Since I bet you won't always have cornhusks on hand, in this recipe you'll shape the corn mixture into little patties that you can simply bake.

FOR THE TAMALES:

3 cups (495 g) thawed frozen corn kernels or fresh corn kernels

¾ cup (113 g) corn flour

1 teaspoon onion powder

1 teaspoon salt

Vegetable oil, to oil baking sheet

FOR THE BRUSCHETTA:

1 large tomato, diced

1 avocado, peeled, pitted, and diced

½ jalapeño pepper, seeded and minced

¼ red onion, minced

1 tablespoon olive oil

Fleur de sel and black pepper, to taste

Juice from ½ lemon or 1 lime

FOR THE CHIPOTLE SAUCE:

½ cup (125 ml) Plant Mayonnaise (page 184)

1 canned chipotle chili, chopped, or ½ teaspoon chipotle chili powder

½ teaspoon maple syrup

½ teaspoon lemon juice

Pinch of salt

FOR SERVING:

Fresh coriander leaves

Lime wedges

Jalapeño pepper, seeded and chopped

FOR THE TAMALES:

1. Preheat the oven to 375°F (190°C).

2. Place all the ingredients except the oil in the bowl of a food processor. Pulse to get a coarse texture.

3. Generously oil a baking sheet. Create 6 to 8 small patties with the corn mixture, transferring them to the prepared baking sheet as you go.

4. Bake for 15 minutes, flipping the patties halfway through. Set aside.

FOR THE BRUSCHETTA:

5. In a large bowl, mix all the ingredients until combined.

FOR THE CHIPOTLE SAUCE:

6. In a small bowl, mix all the ingredients until combined.

TO SERVE:

7. Serve the tamales with the bruschetta and garnish with coriander, lime, and jalapeño, and drizzle some chipotle sauce overtop.

DHAL

SERVES 4 | PREP TIME: 15 MINUTES | COOK TIME: 25 MINUTES

The staple dish of meditation retreats around the world has to be dhal—and for good reason. It's a crowd pleaser! Dhal is a hearty meal, yet you don't feel heavy or sleepy after eating it. It's fragrant, and the spices that flavor the dish can help with digestion.

1. Rinse the lentils and drain.

2. Add the lentils to a saucepan. Add the water and bring to a boil. Lower the heat and simmer for 12 minutes. Set aside.

3. In a second saucepan, over medium-high heat, heat the oil, then add the onions and sweat for 10 minutes, until tender. Add a bit of water, if needed.

4. Add the diced tomatoes, tomato paste, garlic, ginger, curry powder, cumin seeds, turmeric, and coriander.

5. Season with salt and black pepper and keep cooking for a few minutes until fragrant.

6. Stir in the cooked lentils. Garnish with fresh coriander and enjoy.

1 cup (190 g) dry red lentils

2½ cups (625 ml) water

3 tablespoons vegetable oil

2 medium onions, minced

1 tomato, diced

2 tablespoons tomato paste

1 tablespoon minced garlic

1 tablespoon minced fresh ginger

1½ teaspoons curry powder

½ teaspoon cumin seeds

½ teaspoon turmeric

½ teaspoon ground coriander

Salt and black pepper, to taste

Fresh coriander leaves, to garnish

PALAK TOFU

SERVES 4 | **PREP TIME: 15 MINUTES** | **COOK TIME: 20 MINUTES**

Did you know that 350 million Indians are vegetarian? Where do you think they get their protein? Through dishes like palak paneer, an Indian dish from Punjab. This vegan version substitutes tofu for the cheese. To achieve the texture similar to that of Indian paneer cheese, you simply poach the tofu for 2 minutes in water.

1 (350 g) block extra-firm tofu, cubed

1 (5 oz/142 g) package baby spinach

1 (14 oz/398 ml) can coconut milk

2 cloves garlic, minced

1 tablespoon minced fresh ginger

1 tablespoon tomato paste or 2 tablespoons ketchup

1 teaspoon garam masala

1 teaspoon maple syrup

Salt, to taste

1. Bring a pot of water to a boil. Add the tofu and boil for 2 minutes. Drain and set aside.

2. In the same pot, combine the remaining ingredients.

3. Bring to a boil, lower the heat, and simmer for 15 minutes, or until the sauce thickens.

4. Blend until smooth using a hand blender or a stand blender.

5. Return the sauce to the pot and add the tofu.

6. Reheat for 2 minutes, then serve with rice, if desired.

"BUTTER" TOFU

SERVES 4 | PREP TIME: 5 MINUTES | COOK TIME: 20 MINUTES

I think the mind is just like tofu—it absorbs whatever you marinate it in. And in this recipe, the tofu tastes delicious! Here's an Indian curry recipe with a creamy and perfectly spiced sauce you'll want to mop up using warm naan. The secret to this dish is the crispy tofu, which you dredge in corn flour before frying. And who doesn't like crispy things?

1. In a bowl, shake the tofu with the cornstarch to coat.

2. In a large skillet over medium-high heat, heat the vegan butter. Add half of the tofu cubes and fry, turning from time to time, until they're golden brown and crisp.

3. Transfer the tofu cubes to a plate lined with paper towels to drain excess oil. Repeat the steps to fry the remaining tofu cubes, adding more vegan butter as needed. Drain and set aside.

4. In the same skillet over medium heat, add vegan butter if the pan is too dry, and brown the onions for 4 minutes.

5. Stir in the tomato paste, nutritional yeast, sugar, garlic, curry powder, rice vinegar, red pepper flakes, mustard seeds, and turmeric. Keep cooking for 2 minutes.

6. Stir in the coconut milk and bring to a boil.

7. Stir in the frozen peas and tofu.

8. Simmer for 5 minutes, or until the sauce has thickened. Season with salt and pepper. To serve, garnish the butter tofu with microgreens.

1 (450 g) block extra-firm tofu, cubed

¼ cup (32 g) cornstarch

3 tablespoons vegan butter or vegetable oil (plus more as needed)

1 onion, minced

3 tablespoons tomato paste

2 tablespoons nutritional yeast

1 tablespoon cane sugar or maple syrup

2 cloves garlic, minced

1 teaspoon curry powder

1 teaspoon rice vinegar

½ teaspoon red pepper flakes

½ teaspoon mustard seeds

¼ teaspoon turmeric

1 (14 oz/398 ml) can coconut milk

1 cup (160 g) frozen peas

Salt and black pepper, to taste

Microgreens of your choice, to garnish

SPICY PEANUT TOFU

SERVES 4 | **PREP TIME: 20 MINUTES** | **COOK TIME: 10 MINUTES**

I often make this recipe when asked to do a cooking demo because it's quick and it doesn't require an oven or any special equipment or ingredients. It also pleases the whole family. Simply combine all the ingredients in one pan, and voilà! You now have tofu in a rich and spicy peanut butter sauce. Quick and delicious!

2 tablespoons vegetable oil

2 shallots, minced

2 cloves garlic, minced

1 cup (250 ml) vegetable broth

¼ cup (64 g) natural peanut butter

2 tablespoons soy sauce

2 tablespoons ketchup

1 tablespoon maple syrup

½ teaspoon sriracha sauce

1 (450 g) block extra-firm tofu, cubed

Steamed rice, to serve

1. In a large saucepan over medium-high heat, heat the oil.

2. Add the shallots and garlic and sauté for 2 minutes.

3. Add the vegetable broth, peanut butter, soy sauce, ketchup, maple syrup, and sriracha sauce and stir thoroughly to combine.

4. Add the tofu, bring to a boil, then simmer until the sauce is creamy. Serve over steamed rice.

GENERAL TSO'S TOFU

SERVES 4 | **PREP TIME: 20 MINUTES** | **COOK TIME: 15 MINUTES**

Do you want to eat less meat? Start by replacing it in recipes you know and love, such as General Tso's chicken. Simply swap the chicken with tofu: it's so simple, yet so good! This recipe is always hugely successful with meat eaters. Seriously, look up "crowd-pleaser" in the dictionary and you're likely to find a picture of this recipe. It's a guaranteed hit!

1. In a bowl, shake the tofu with the cornstarch to coat.

2. In a large skillet over medium-high heat, heat the oil. Add half of the tofu cubes and fry, turning from time to time, until they're golden brown and crisp. Transfer the tofu cubes to a plate lined with paper towels to drain excess oil. Repeat the steps to fry the remaining tofu cubes, adding more oil as needed. Drain and set aside.

3. In the same skillet, cook the garlic and ginger together for 1 minute. Add more oil, if needed.

4. Add the vegetable broth, green onions, maple syrup, soy sauce, ketchup, and sriracha sauce, and stir to combine. Simmer for a few minutes to thicken, then stir the fried tofu into the sauce to reheat it.

5. Serve over steamed rice and garnish with sliced green onions and sesame seeds.

1 (450 g) block extra-firm tofu, cubed

¼ cup (32 g) cornstarch

3 tablespoons vegetable oil, plus more as needed

2 cloves garlic, minced

1 tablespoon minced fresh ginger

¾ cup (180 ml) vegetable broth

3 green onions, minced

2 tablespoons maple syrup

2 tablespoons soy sauce

2 tablespoons ketchup

1 teaspoon sriracha sauce or chili paste

Steamed rice, to serve

Sliced green onions, to garnish

Sesame seeds, to garnish

PAD THAI

Thai cuisine is probably one of the most exciting in the world, and certainly one of my favorites. Why? Because Thai dishes rely on the interaction between four tastes: salty, sweet, spicy, and sour. When the balance is achieved, the result is spectacular! I discovered this vegan pad thai in Bangkok at a cooking class that was held in a very nice vegetarian restaurant. I fell in love with the easy recipe and adapted it so that everybody can cook it at home. I hope you like it!

5 ounces (140 g) rice noodles

½ block (227 g) extra-firm tofu, cubed

¼ cup (32 g) cornstarch

4 tablespoons vegetable oil, divided

2 carrots, cut into matchsticks or grated

1 tomato, diced

2 shallots, minced

2 green onions, thinly sliced

2 teaspoons minced garlic

¼ cup (60 ml) soy sauce

¼ cup (50 g) cane sugar or granulated sugar

1 teaspoon sambal oelek, or chili flakes, to taste

2 cups (150 g) bean sprouts

½ cup (75 g) crushed peanuts

2 teaspoons rice vinegar

Salt and black pepper, to taste

1. Add the rice noodles to a large bowl of boiling water, then let them soak for a few minutes to rehydrate. Drain and set aside.

2. In a bowl, dredge the tofu cubes in the cornstarch.

3. In a wok over medium-high heat, heat 2 tablespoons of the oil, then add the tofu and fry until golden. Remove from the wok and set aside.

4. In the same wok over medium-high heat, heat the remaining 2 tablespoons oil, then add the carrots, tomatoes, shallots, green onions, and garlic, and cook for 5 minutes.

5. Add the soy sauce, sugar, and sambal oelek. Stir to combine.

6. Add the drained rice noodles, bean sprouts, fried tofu, crushed peanuts, and rice vinegar. Keep cooking for 3 minutes, stirring constantly. Season with salt and black pepper. Enjoy.

EGGPLANT GREEN CURRY

SERVES 2 | PREP TIME: 20 MINUTES | COOK TIME: 25 MINUTES

Green curry is one of my favorite dishes. I had some every day when I was in Thailand. The secret to this dish is to find the right curry paste. You will typically find it canned in Asian grocery stores. The common ingredients found in green curry paste are lime leaves, galangal (Thai ginger), and lemongrass. It's fragrant and slightly spicy, and it goes wonderfully with eggplant. You can add small extra-firm tofu cubes at the end of the cooking process to make it a complete meal.

1. In a saucepan over high heat, heat the oil, then add the eggplant, red bell peppers, and onions. Sauté for 5 minutes.

2. Add the curry paste. Stir to combine, then keep cooking for 2 minutes.

3. Stir in the coconut milk, then add the maple syrup and kaffir lime leaves.

4. Bring to a boil, lower the heat, and simmer for 15 minutes, or until the vegetables are tender.

5. Adjust the seasoning, if needed, and serve over steamed rice.

¼ cup (60 ml) vegetable oil

1 eggplant (about 500 g), cut into large cubes

1 red bell pepper, diced

1 onion, minced

1 tablespoon green curry paste

1½ cups (375 ml) canned coconut milk

2 teaspoons maple syrup or cane sugar

2 kaffir lime leaves

Salt, to taste

Steamed rice, to serve

PAD KEE MAO

SERVES 2 | PREP TIME: 15 MINUTES | COOK TIME: 20 MINUTES

The literal translation of "pad kee mao" is "drunken noodles," the theory being that these spicy noodles go perfectly with an ice-cold beer; they're also a great cure for a hangover. As a Buddhist, I don't drink alcohol . . . or not much, anyway. I do admit that, with age, I have found that I can't party like I used to. So instead, I party in a different way: I have a cup of tea and go to bed at 9:00 p.m.

¼ cup (60 ml) vegetable oil

1 head broccoli, cut into florets

1 red bell pepper, sliced

1 (450 g) block extra-firm tofu, diced

¾ cup (180 ml) vegetable broth

¼ cup (60 ml) ketchup

¼ cup (60 ml) soy sauce

¼ cup (60 ml) maple syrup

¼ teaspoon red pepper flakes or ½ teaspoon sriracha sauce

12 oz (340 g) cooked Asian noodles, pad thai noodles, or spaghetti

Salt, to taste

3 green onions, minced, to garnish

1. In a large skillet over high heat, heat the oil, then add the vegetables and tofu and sauté for 5 to 10 minutes.

2. Add the vegetable broth, ketchup, soy sauce, maple syrup, and red pepper flakes.

3. Add the noodles and keep cooking until the sauce has reduced and thickened. (If you're using spaghetti, add it after the sauce has thickened to avoid overcooking the pasta.). Add salt to taste.

4. Garnish with the green onions before serving.

SSÄMS

SERVES 4 | PREP TIME: 1 HOUR | COOK TIME: 35 MINUTES | REST TIME: 26 HOURS (KIMCHI) PLUS
15 MINUTES (RICE) | REFRIGERATION TIME: 24 HOURS (KIMCHI)

Ssäm is a popular Korean dish. The name of the dish means "wrapped," and once you know that, the dish becomes pretty self-explanatory: it's food wrapped in lettuce. Ssäms are a warm and fun dish to serve to a group. I love shareable food. I simply place the plates of food in the center of the table and let everyone help themselves. If you like sushi, you'll love ssäms. Plus, the peanut sauce is so good, you'll want to eat every last drop!

FOR THE KIMCHI:

1 Chinese (napa) cabbage (about 850 g)

3 tablespoons salt

3 cloves garlic, minced

2 tablespoons minced fresh ginger

1 tablespoon cane sugar or granulated sugar

4 carrots, thinly sliced (about 200 g)

6 green onions, thinly sliced

½ cup (50 g) Korean chili powder

½ cup (125 ml) water

¼ cup (60 ml) soy sauce

FOR THE RICE:

1 cup (225 g) sushi rice

1½ cups (375 ml) water, or per rice package instructions

½ teaspoon salt

1 tablespoon rice vinegar

1 tablespoon maple syrup or agave syrup

FOR THE TEMPEH:

1 (8½ oz/240 g) package tempeh

1 cup (250 ml) vegetable broth

2 tablespoons toasted sesame oil

2 tablespoons vegan hoisin sauce

FOR THE SATAY SAUCE:

1 tablespoon vegetable oil

2 cloves garlic, minced

¼ cup (60 ml) vegetable broth

2 tablespoons vegan hoisin sauce

1 tablespoon maple syrup

1 tablespoon natural peanut butter

1 teaspoon sambal oelek

TO SERVE:

8 to 12 lettuce leaves

Sliced avocado

Microgreens

FOR THE KIMCHI:

1. Chop the cabbage into 1½-inch (4 cm) pieces.

2. Transfer the cabbage to a large bowl, then sprinkle with the salt. Toss to combine and let rest for 2 hours.

3. Drain the cabbage and rinse thoroughly. Set aside.

4. In a mortar, pound the garlic with the ginger and sugar.

5. Transfer the mixture to a large stainless-steel bowl, then add the cabbage, carrots, green onions, Korean chili powder, water, and soy sauce. Mix thoroughly.

recipe continues

6. Transfer the mixture to clean glass jars, close the jars tightly, and leave to ferment in a dark spot at room temperature for 24 hours.

7. Transfer the jars to the refrigerator and leave to ferment for 24 hours more. The kimchi will keep refrigerated for up to 3 weeks.

FOR THE RICE:

8. Rinse the rice under cold running water, then transfer to a large pot. Stir in the water, then bring to a boil. Cover, lower the heat to the minimum, and gently simmer for 15 to 20 minutes, or until all the water is absorbed.

9. Remove from the heat and let the rice rest, covered, for 15 minutes.

10. Add the salt, rice vinegar, and maple syrup. Stir to combine, then let cool.

FOR THE TEMPEH:

11. Thinly slice the tempeh and transfer to a skillet.

12. In a bowl, whisk together the vegetable broth, toasted sesame oil, and hoisin sauce.

13. Pour the marinade over the tempeh slices and bring to a boil over high heat.

14. Boil until all the liquid is absorbed, about 10 minutes, flipping the slices halfway through. Set aside.

FOR THE SATAY SAUCE:

15. In a large skillet over medium heat, heat the oil, then add the garlic and cook for 2 minutes.

16. Add the remaining ingredients, bring to a simmer, and cook until the sauce has thickened. Set aside.

TO SERVE:

17. Spoon some rice over the lettuce leaves, then add a slice of tempeh, drizzle with satay sauce, and garnish with kimchi, avocados, and microgreens. Fold the lettuce leaves over the filling and enjoy.

The Best Hummus (page 150)

SNACKS
AND SIDES

COCONUT MATCHA ENERGY BALLS

MAKES 24 BALLS | **PREP TIME: 15 MINUTES** | **REFRIGERATION TIME: 12 HOURS**

Some people ask me, "What do you do to have so much energy?" My answer: "I drink lots of coffee." But there's a limit to how much coffee you can drink in a day . . . unfortunately. So I treat myself to an energy ball—and yes, sometimes I double my energy dose and have it with a cup of coffee!

1. Pour boiling water over the cashews and soak for 10 minutes. Drain.

2. In a food processor, combine the cashews, dates, shredded coconut, coconut oil, matcha tea, and salt.

3. Using your hands or a cookie scoop, shape the mixture into small balls, then roll them in shredded coconut and, if you like, crushed pistachios.

4. Refrigerate overnight, then bring to room temperature before eating.

½ cup (71 g) cashews

2 cups (250 g) small pitted dates

2 cups (100 g) unsweetened shredded coconut (plus more for rolling)

2 tablespoons coconut oil

2 teaspoons powdered matcha tea

Pinch of salt

Crushed pistachios, for rolling (optional)

Tip: The energy balls will keep refrigerated for up to 1 week or frozen for up to 3 months—they can be eaten frozen too.

KALE CHIPS

SERVES 4 | **PREP TIME: 15 MINUTES** | **COOK TIME: 15 TO 20 MINUTES**

The secret of this recipe is to dry the kale leaves thoroughly before coating them with the flavorings. It's worth it!

1 bunch (about 150 g) kale
2 tablespoons olive oil
2 tablespoons nutritional yeast
½ teaspoon fleur de sel

1. Preheat the oven to 325°F (160°C).

2. Cut the thick stalks out of each kale leaf.

3. Coarsely tear the kale leaves.

4. Clean the kale leaf pieces under cold running water, then dry thoroughly (ideally using a salad spinner).

5. Transfer the kale to a large bowl.

6. Add the oil, nutritional yeast, and fleur de sel. Toss to coat the kale with the flavorings.

7. Spread the kale on a baking sheet.

8. Bake for 15 to 20 minutes, or until the leaves are crisp. Enjoy.

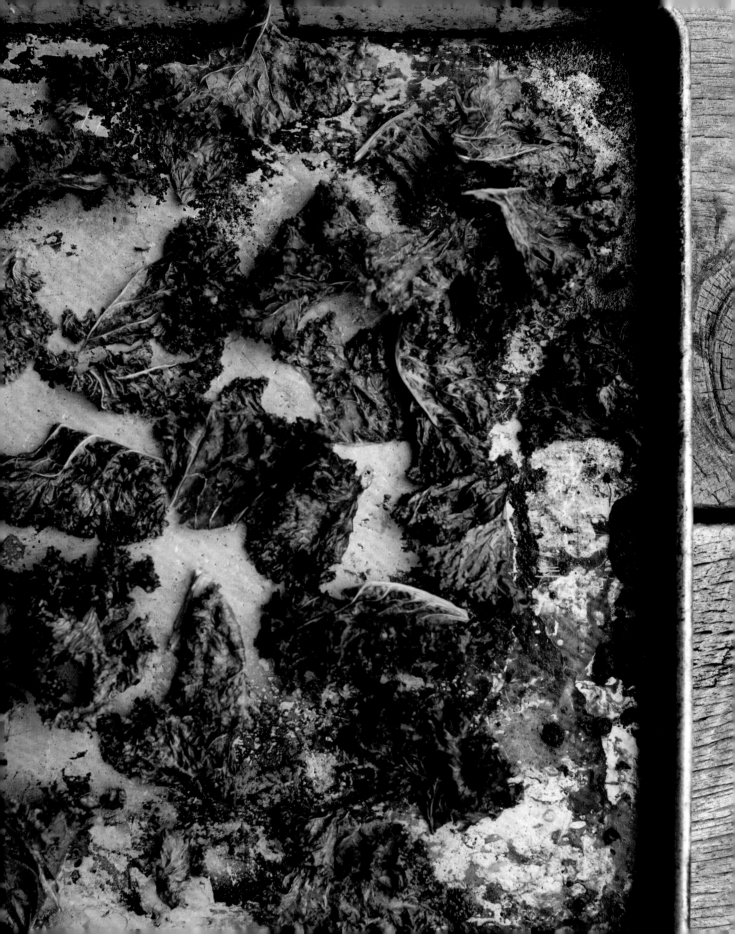

THE BEST HUMMUS

MAKES ABOUT 3 CUPS (750 ML) | **PREP TIME: 15 MINUTES**

Why buy store-bought hummus when this recipe, and all the variations, take it to new heights.

1 (19 oz/540 ml) can chickpeas, rinsed and drained

⅓ cup (80 ml) water

3 tablespoons tahini or natural peanut butter

2 tablespoons olive oil (plus 1 tablespoon, to garnish)

Juice from ½ lemon

1 clove garlic, minced

1 teaspoon ground cumin

⅛ teaspoon cayenne pepper

Salt, to taste

Smoked paprika, to garnish

Pita bread, to serve

Tip: Hummus will keep refrigerated for up to 4 days.

1. In a food processor, grind the chickpeas together with the water, tahini, oil, lemon juice, garlic, cumin, cayenne pepper, and salt until the mixture is smooth.

2. Transfer the hummus to a serving plate. Garnish with a drizzle of olive oil and sprinkle with smoked paprika. Serve with pita bread.

VARIATIONS:

To make a flavored hummus, just add your preferred flavoring in step 1, reserving some to garnish:

CARAMELIZED ONION HUMMUS:
Basic recipe plus ¼ cup (60 ml) caramelized onions

SUN-DRIED TOMATO HUMMUS:
Basic recipe plus ¼ cup (60 ml) sun-dried tomatoes

SPICY JALAPEÑO HUMMUS:
Basic recipe plus 2 tablespoons canned jalapeño

ROASTED CHICKPEAS

SERVES 2 | **PREP TIME: 10 MINUTES** | **COOK TIME: 30 TO 45 MINUTES**

Yesterday, I tried not thinking about food for an hour. It was the longest five minutes of my life! I'm one of those people who invariably answers in the affirmative when asked, "Are you hungry?" It doesn't matter what time it is—day or night. It's actually hard to find a picture of me without my mouth full. When I'm hungry, I'm vulnerable, so it's easy for me to indulge in chocolate or cookies as if my life depended on it. This is why I always make sure to have a healthy snack on hand, and these delicious roasted chickpeas fit the bill perfectly.

1. Preheat the oven to 375°F (190°C).

2. In a large skillet over high heat, heat the oil, then add the chickpeas and sauté for 2 minutes.

3. Add the remaining ingredients and mix to combine.

4. Transfer to a baking sheet.

5. Bake for 30 to 45 minutes, or until the chickpeas are crispy. Let cool slightly, then enjoy.

2 tablespoons vegetable oil

1 cup (175 g) canned chickpeas, rinsed and drained

1 teaspoon maple syrup

1 teaspoon paprika

1 teaspoon ground coriander

1 teaspoon ground cumin

1 teaspoon garlic powder

⅛ teaspoon cayenne pepper

Fleur de sel

Tip: The roasted chickpeas will keep in an airtight container at room temperature for up to 4 weeks.

BROILED BRUSSELS SPROUTS

SERVES 4 | PREP TIME: 20 MINUTES | COOK TIME: 20 MINUTES

My travels in Southeast Asia taught me that a dish with well-balanced flavors can be exceptional—even if it's made with Brussels sprouts. This combination of sweet and salty ingredients combined with bitter Brussels sprouts, plus a little heat, is fantastic. The flavors will just burst in your mouth.

FOR THE BRUSSELS SPROUTS:

4 cups (500 g) Brussels sprouts, halved

2 tablespoons vegetable oil

FOR THE SAUCE:

2 tablespoons vegetable oil

4 green onions, minced

¼ cup (60 ml) soy sauce

¼ cup (60 ml) maple syrup

1 clove garlic, minced

¼ teaspoon red pepper flakes

FOR THE BRUSSELS SPROUTS:

1. Preheat the oven to broil.

2. In a large pot, bring 8 cups (2 L) water to a boil, then add the Brussels sprouts. Boil for 3 minutes.

3. Remove the sprouts from the water, pat dry, then transfer to a bowl. Drizzle the Brussel sprouts with the oil and stir to coat.

4. Spread the Brussels sprouts on a baking sheet, then broil for 3 to 4 minutes.

5. Flip the Brussels sprouts, then continue to broil until they're golden brown in spots.

FOR THE SAUCE:

6. In a small saucepan over medium heat, heat the oil. Add the green onions and sweat for 2 minutes.

7. Stir in the soy sauce, maple syrup, garlic, and red pepper flakes. Simmer for 5 minutes.

8. Drizzle the sauce over the Brussels sprouts and serve.

SZECHUAN ROASTED GREEN BEANS

SERVES 4 | **PREP TIME: 20 MINUTES** | **COOK TIME: 10 MINUTES**

A classic ingredient in French cuisine, green beans are one of those vegetables that deserves to be rediscovered. I've given them an Asian twist by roasting them and drizzling them with toasted sesame oil, which adds a surprising kick.

1. Fill a large pot with water, then bring to a boil.

2. Add the green beans, wait for the water to come back to a boil, then cook for 1 minute.

3. Drain the beans, pat dry, then transfer to a large bowl.

4. Preheat the oven to broil.

5. While the oven is preheating, drizzle the beans with toasted sesame oil, generously season with salt, and toss to combine.

6. Spread the beans on a baking sheet, then broil for a few minutes, just until the beans start turning golden brown in spots. Toss the beans, then broil for a few minutes more.

7. While the beans are broiling, place the maple syrup, cider vinegar, and sambal oelek in a small saucepan. Bring to a boil, then simmer until the mixture is syrupy.

8. Remove the beans from the oven and transfer them to a large serving bowl. Add the hot dressing.

9. Toss to combine, then garnish with sesame seeds before serving.

10 cups (1 kg) green beans, trimmed

2 tablespoons toasted sesame oil

Salt

¼ cup (60 ml) maple syrup

2 tablespoons cider vinegar

1 teaspoon sambal oelek

2 tablespoons sesame seeds, to garnish

IMPERIAL ROLLS

MAKES 12 ROLLS | PREP TIME: 1 HOUR | COOK TIME: 20 MINUTES |
REFRIGERATION TIME: 30 MINUTES (FOR FILLING AND SAUCE)

What's the difference between chore and leisure? The time you devote to it. This is why I love cooking when I'm not in a hurry, such as on the weekends. If I have to spend more than 20 minutes making a recipe, I'll plan on freezing some of it by doubling the quantities. These delicious spring rolls are a great make-ahead treat; they can be frozen either raw or cooked.

FOR THE FILLING:

¼ cup (60 ml) vegetable oil

8 cups (500 g) shredded Chinese (napa) cabbage

3 portobello mushrooms, thinly sliced

2 carrots, grated

1 cup (175 g) cooked rice vermicelli

2 cloves garlic, minced

1 tablespoon cane sugar or granulated sugar

1 tablespoon rice vinegar

1 tablespoon soy sauce

2 teaspoons toasted sesame oil

1 teaspoon cornstarch whisked into 2 tablespoons water

Salt, to taste

FOR THE SAUCE:

⅔ cup (160 ml) water

¼ cup (50 g) cane sugar or granulated sugar

⅛ teaspoon red pepper flakes

1 tablespoon rice vinegar

TO ASSEMBLE:

1 tablespoon all-purpose flour

¼ cup (60 ml) water

12 sheets spring roll pastry (8½-inch/22 cm squares)

Vegetable oil, for frying

FOR THE FILLING:

1. In a large skillet over medium heat, heat the oil, then add the cabbage, mushrooms, and carrots. Cook for 8 to 10 minutes, or until tender.

2. Add the rice vermicelli, garlic, sugar, rice vinegar, soy sauce, and toasted sesame oil. Stir to combine.

3. Stir in the cornstarch mixture and keep cooking, stirring continuously, for 2 minutes.

4. Season with salt and remove from the heat.

5. Transfer the mixture to a large bowl and let cool slightly. Refrigerate until the mixture is cool.

FOR THE SAUCE:

6. In a saucepan, combine the water, sugar, and red pepper flakes.

7. Boil for 10 minutes over medium-high heat to thicken the sauce.

8. Remove from the heat. Stir in the rice vinegar. Let cool, then refrigerate until ready to use.

TO ASSEMBLE:

9. In a deep fryer, heat the oil to 350°F (175°C). Line a baking sheet with paper towels.

10. In a small bowl, whisk the flour and water together.

11. To create a roll, set 1 pastry sheet diagonally on a work surface. Spoon about ¼ cup (60 ml) of the filling in a horizontal line in the center of the pastry sheet. Fold the bottom tip of the pastry over the filling. Fold the left and right tips over the filling. Tightly roll to enclose the filling and create a cylinder-shaped roll. To seal the roll, brush some of the flour and water mixture along the edge of the top tip of the pastry sheet, then fold it shut. Repeat these steps to create all the rolls.

12. Fry the rolls, 6 at a time, for 4 to 5 minutes, or until golden brown. Transfer to the paper towel–lined baking sheet to drain. Serve the imperial rolls with the dipping sauce.

Chocolate Cake (page 178)

DESSERT

CHOCOLATE LAVA CAKES

SERVES 4 | PREP TIME: 20 MINUTES | COOK TIME: 10 TO 15 MINUTES |
REFRIGERATION TIME: 30 MINUTES AND UP TO 4 DAYS

Have you ever wondered what a cloud tastes like? I think it might be this cake, which has chocolate . . . and chickpeas in it! Who knew chickpeas and chocolate could work together so well? This recipe will blow your mind. The secret is to bake the cakes just before serving them. The exterior of the cakes should be set, but the centers still runny. You'll have to keep a close eye on them during baking, but believe me, it's worth it!

1. Using 2 tablespoons of the coconut oil, grease 4 ramekins (½ cup/125 ml capacity), then lightly dust with flour.

2. In a saucepan over low heat, melt the chocolate and ⅔ cup (160 ml) coconut oil. Set aside.

3. Place the chickpeas in a blender. Add the plant milk, sugar, baking powder, salt, and vanilla, then blend to combine.

4. Add the flour and the melted chocolate mixture, then blend until you reach a smooth consistency.

5. Divide the batter between the prepared ramekins, then refrigerate for at least 30 minutes or up to 4 days maximum.

6. When you're ready to serve, preheat the oven to 375°F (190°C).

7. Remove the cakes from the fridge and bake immediately for 5 to 10 minutes, or until the edges are set but the centers are still runny.

8. Remove the cakes by flipping the ramekins upside down over serving plates. Dust with powdered sugar. Serve warm.

⅔ cup (160 ml) coconut oil (plus 2 tablespoons to grease the ramekins)

½ cup (64 g) all-purpose flour (plus more for dusting the ramekins)

4 oz (110 g) 85% cacao vegan chocolate

1½ cups (240 g) canned chickpeas, rinsed and drained

1 cup (250 ml) plant milk

1 cup (200 g) cane sugar or granulated sugar

1 teaspoon baking powder

1 teaspoon salt

½ teaspoon vanilla extract

Powdered sugar, for dusting

BAKLAVA

SERVES 8 | PREP TIME: 20 MINUTES | COOK TIME: 35 MINUTES

I have a secret: I was a bit selfish when creating this baklava recipe. It's true. I made it just to treat myself, before even thinking of giving it to anyone else! I couldn't help myself; it is one of my favorite desserts, after all. So how do you make baklava without using honey? Use maple syrup!

FOR THE SYRUP:

1 cup (250 ml) maple syrup

½ cup (125 ml) water

⅓ cup (73 g) packed brown sugar

1 tablespoon lemon juice

¼ teaspoon ground cinnamon

FOR THE FLAKY PASTRY:

1 cup (142 g) shelled pistachios

1 cup (142 g) pecans

5 sheets phyllo pastry

¼ cup (60 ml) vegetable oil

FOR THE SYRUP:

1. In a saucepan, combine all the ingredients and bring to a boil. Simmer for 2 minutes, then let cool to room temperature. Set aside.

FOR THE FLAKY PASTRY:

2. Preheat the oven to 325°F (160°C).

3. In a food processor, coarsely chop the pistachios and pecans by pulsing for a few seconds at a time. Set aside.

4. Lay a sheet of phyllo pastry on your work surface, then brush it all over with oil.

5. Cover with a second sheet, then brush that too all over with oil. Repeat the process with the remaining 3 sheets of phyllo pastry.

6. Cut the layered pastry in half. Place half in the bottom of a 9 × 13-inch (23 × 33 cm) baking dish.

7. Sprinkle with two-thirds of the chopped nuts.

8. Cover with the second half of layered pastry. Sprinkle with the remaining nuts. Cut into squares, then bake for 30 minutes, or until the pastry is golden brown.

9. Let cool. If desired, layer 2 squares to double the height of the baklava. Spoon some of the syrup over the squares and serve.

DATE SQUARES

SERVES 12 | PREP TIME: 20 MINUTES | COOK TIME: 55 MINUTES TO 1 HOUR, 10 MINUTES

What's cheap, sweet, and healthy? Me! Just kidding. I'm really talking about dates; they are versatile but also somewhat mysterious because we hardly ever see them in their original form. They're always dried. In the Middle East, dates are frequently used in savory recipes, but my grandmother liked to use them to make sweet date squares. Proof that dates are versatile!

1. Preheat the oven to 350°F (175°C).

2. Spread the chopped pecans on a baking sheet and toast for 5 minutes. Set aside.

3. In a saucepan, combine the dates, water, maple syrup, and lemon juice. Bring to a boil, then lower the heat and simmer until the liquid is fully absorbed, about 20 minutes. Set aside.

4. In a large bowl, combine the toasted pecans, flour, rolled oats, brown sugar, cane sugar, baking soda, and salt.

5. Add the melted vegan butter and mix until fully incorporated.

6. Pour two-thirds of the mixture into a buttered 9-inch (23 cm) square baking dish.

7. Spread the date mixture over the crust, level the top, then sprinkle the remaining flour and oats mixture over top.

8. Bake for 30 to 45 minutes, then let cool for a few minutes.

9. Cut into squares and enjoy.

1 cup (142 g) coarsely chopped pecans

4 cups (500 g) pitted dates, coarsely chopped

1⅔ cups (410 ml) water

¼ cup (60 ml) maple syrup

1 tablespoon lemon juice

1½ cups (190 g) all-purpose flour

1 cup (80 g) rolled oats

½ cup (110 g) packed brown sugar

¼ cup (50 g) cane sugar or granulated sugar

1 teaspoon baking soda

1 teaspoon salt

⅔ cup (160 ml) melted vegan butter (plus more for baking dish)

CINNAMON BUNS

MAKES 9 BUNS | PREP TIME: 40 MINUTES |
COOK TIME: 25 TO 30 MINUTES | REST TIME: 1 HOUR, 30 MINUTES

Cooking is a great teacher: it can teach you patience, concentration, balance, compassion, and mindfulness. It can also help you find love! It worked for me: I'm happily married, and I spend most of my time in the kitchen. I knew what I was getting into when she added "and I'll cook for you forever after" to *my* marriage vows. What I didn't know was that I would also have to wash the dishes—evidently that was in the fine print!

FOR THE BUNS:

1 cup (250 ml) plant milk

1 (2¼ tsp/7 g) package active-dry yeast

¼ cup (50 g) cane sugar or granulated sugar

¼ cup (60 ml) melted vegan butter (plus ¼ cup/60 ml to brush over the dough)

1 teaspoon salt

2½ cups (310 g) all-purpose flour (plus more as needed, and for flouring the work surface)

½ cup (110 g) packed brown sugar

1½ teaspoons ground cinnamon

FOR THE GLAZE:

2 tablespoons coconut oil

1¼ cups (150 g) powdered sugar

3 tablespoons hot water

FOR THE BUNS:

1. Preheat the oven to 350°F (175°C).

2. Heat the plant milk in the microwave or in a skillet for 30 seconds to 1 minute, until it's warm.

3. In a large bowl, combine the warm milk and the yeast.

4. Let rest for 5 minutes, until the top of the mixture is frothy.

5. Add the sugar, ¼ cup (60 ml) melted butter, and salt. Stir to combine.

6. Add the flour and knead for 1 minute, or until the mixture comes together in a sticky ball. Add more flour, if needed.

7. Cover the bowl with a clean damp kitchen towel and let rest for 1 hour at room temperature.

8. Transfer the dough to a floured work surface and roll out to a 12 × 18-inch (30 × 45 cm) rectangle.

9. Brush the surface of the dough with the remaining ¼ cup (60 ml) butter.

10. Sprinkle with brown sugar, then with the cinnamon.

11. Roll the dough lengthwise, then slice into 9 rounds of equal thickness.

12. Set the rounds flat on a buttered or parchment paper–lined baking sheet.

13. Let rest for 30 minutes to allow the buns to rise further.

14. Bake for 20 to 30 minutes.

FOR THE GLAZE:

15. In a saucepan over low heat, melt the coconut oil. Stir in the powdered sugar and water.

16. Remove the buns from the oven and let cool for a few minutes. Drizzle with the glaze and enjoy.

TAPIOCA PUDDING

SERVES 4 | PREP TIME: 10 MINUTES | COOK TIME: 30 MINUTES | REFRIGERATION TIME: 2 HOURS

This recipe was inspired by the bubble tea you can find in Chinatown shops and cafés. Coconut and tapioca make a great pair, and kidney beans add something surprising to this recipe. True story: my doctor—who is also my beautiful wife—pointed out that tapioca is super-nutritious, which is one of the reasons it is often served in hospitals.

1. Place all the ingredients except the red kidney beans in a saucepan.

2. Bring to a boil, stirring continuously, then lower the heat to the minimum. Gently simmer for 30 minutes, stirring regularly to make sure the tapioca doesn't stick to the bottom of the pan.

3. Spoon some of the tapioca into the bottom of 4 ramekins. Divide the red kidney beans between the ramekins, then top with more tapioca. Garnish with the remaining kidney beans. Refrigerate for at least 2 hours before serving.

1½ cups (375 ml) plant milk

1 (14 oz/398 ml) can coconut milk

½ cup (80 g) tapioca pearls, rinsed and drained

¼ cup (60 ml) maple syrup

⅛ teaspoon salt

½ can (9½ oz/270 ml) red kidney beans, rinsed and drained, divided

LEMON MERINGUE PIE

MAKES 1 PIE | PREP TIME: 30 MINUTES | COOK TIME: 35 MINUTES | REFRIGERATION TIME: 1 HOUR

Every fruit has its own personality. Banana: funny. Apple: healthy. Lemon: makes wonderful desserts. But let's face it—who would've ever eaten lemon if it weren't for sugar? This is proof that opposites attract! Don't be so bitter, lemon, we love you . . . as long as you bring sugar along.

FOR THE PLANT MERINGUE:

1 cup (250 ml) aquafaba (the liquid from a 19 oz/540 ml can of chickpeas)

¼ cup (30 g) powdered sugar

⅛ teaspoon cream of tartar (optional)

FOR THE CRUST:

1 cup (125 g) all-purpose flour

1 cup (96 g) almond flour

½ cup (125 ml) coconut oil

⅓ cup (70 g) granulated sugar

¼ teaspoon salt

FOR THE FILLING:

3 cups (750 ml) canned coconut milk

¾ cup (150 g) granulated sugar

½ cup (64 g) cornstarch

Zest from 2 lemons

⅓ cup (80 ml) lemon juice

1 teaspoon powdered agar-agar

½ teaspoon turmeric

¼ teaspoon salt

FOR THE PLANT MERINGUE:

1. In a saucepan, gently simmer the aquafaba for 10 to 15 minutes to reduce. (This will allow the aquafaba to whip more easily.)

2. Transfer the reduced aquafaba to a large bowl and let cool for 5 minutes. Add the powdered sugar and cream of tartar (if using), then beat for 5 minutes, or until the meringue is thick. Refrigerate.

FOR THE CRUST:

3. Preheat the oven to 350°F (175°C).

4. In a large bowl, add the flour, almond flour, coconut oil, sugar, and salt, and mix until you reach a sandy texture.

5. Using your fingers, press the mixture into the bottom of a 10-inch (25 cm) round cake pan with a removable bottom.

6. Bake for 20 minutes, or until the crust is golden. Let cool.

FOR THE FILLING:

7. In a saucepan off the heat, whisk together all the ingredients.

8. Set the saucepan over high heat and bring to a boil, stirring continuously. Simmer for 1 minute, then remove the saucepan from the heat.

TO SERVE:

9. Pour the filling into the crust and transfer to the refrigerator to let cool for at least 1 hour. Remove the pie from the pan, and top it with the meringue right before serving.

LEMON POPPYSEED CAKE

MAKES 1 CAKE | PREP TIME: 30 MINUTES | COOK TIME: 40 TO 45 MINUTES

My mom used to make this cake when we had guests, and every time I bake it, I think about her. It's so delicious: a lemon cake with a lemon frosting. Have I told you how much of a lemon lover I am?

FOR THE CAKE:

1. Preheat the oven to 350°F (175°C).

2. Grease an 8-inch (20 cm) round cake pan. Line it with parchment paper. Set aside.

3. In a bowl, whisk together the flour, almond flour, sugar, baking powder, and salt.

4. Add the plant milk, vegetable oil, poppyseeds, and lemon zest and juice. Mix until the batter is smooth.

5. Pour the batter into the prepared pan and bake for 40 to 45 minutes, or until a toothpick inserted in the center of the cake comes out clean.

6. Let the cake cool for 15 minutes. Remove from the baking dish, and let cool completely on a wire rack.

FOR THE GLAZE:

7. In a bowl, whisk together the powdered sugar, melted coconut oil, and lemon juice.

8. Pour the glaze over the cooled cake. Garnish with a few lemon slices and let set for a few minutes before serving.

FOR THE CAKE:

2 cups (250 g) all-purpose flour

1 cup (96 g) almond flour

1 cup (200 g) cane sugar or granulated sugar

2 teaspoons baking powder

1 teaspoon salt

1¼ cups (310 ml) plant milk

½ cup (125 ml) vegetable oil

¼ cup (36 g) poppyseeds

Zest and juice from 1 lemon

FOR THE GLAZE:

1¼ cups (150 g) powdered sugar

2 tablespoons melted coconut oil

2 tablespoons lemon juice

Thinly sliced lemon, to garnish

Tip: For a smaller serving size, just bake the batter in muffin tins instead.

COOKIES, TWO WAYS

(FOR EACH VARIATION) MAKES 12 COOKIES | PREP TIME: 15 MINUTES | COOK TIME: 10 TO 12 MINUTES

When I arrive at the meditation center to cook, I am always greeted with "Are you going to make us cookies?" And then: "Are the cookies ready yet?" Followed by: "Can I take two?" There is just something about cookies that makes us feel like kids again (ahem, it's the sugar).

PEANUT BUTTER COOKIES

1⅔ cups (210 g) all-purpose flour

1 teaspoon baking soda

1 teaspoon salt

¾ cup (192 g) natural peanut
butter (see tip)

⅔ cup (160 ml) solid coconut oil

⅓ cup (80 ml) plant milk

⅓ cup (73 g) packed brown sugar

⅓ cup (67 g) cane sugar or
granulated sugar

1 teaspoon vanilla extract

1. Preheat the oven to 375°F (190°C).

2. In a large bowl, combine the flour, baking soda, and salt. Set aside.

3. In a second bowl, beat the remaining ingredients together for 1 to 2 minutes.

4. Mix the dry ingredients into the wet ingredients.

5. Use an ice-cream scoop to portion the dough and drop the mounds onto a baking sheet lined with parchment paper or a silicone mat.

6. Flatten the cookies with the back of a fork.

7. Bake for 10 to 12 minutes, then let the cookies cool completely on the baking sheet. Enjoy.

Tip: It's essential to use high-quality natural peanut butter in this recipe. The taste of the cookies depends on it! Also, make sure to mix in the excess oil that comes up to the surface of natural peanut butter before measuring it.

DOUBLE CHOCOLATE COOKIES

2 cups (250 g) all-purpose flour

1 cup (96 g) almond flour

¼ cup (21 g) cocoa powder

1 teaspoon baking soda

1 teaspoon salt

1 cup (227 g) vegan butter

1 cup (200 g) cane sugar or
granulated sugar

½ cup (110 g) packed brown
sugar

1 teaspoon vanilla extract

⅔ cup (100 g) coarsely chopped
semisweet vegan chocolate

⅓ cup (80 ml) plant milk

1. Preheat the oven to 375°F (190°C).

2. In a bowl, whisk together the flour, almond flour, cocoa powder, baking soda, and salt. Set aside.

3. In a second bowl, beat the butter, cane sugar, brown sugar, and vanilla for 5 minutes, or until the mixture is fluffy.

4. Mix the dry ingredients into the wet ingredients.

5. Add the chopped chocolate and plant milk and stir to combine.

6. Use an ice-cream scoop to portion the dough and drop the mounds onto a baking sheet lined with parchment paper or a silicone mat.

7. Flatten the cookies with the back of a fork.

8. Bake for 10 minutes, then let the cookies cool completely on the baking sheet. Enjoy.

"Today, I will live in the moment. Unless the moment is unpleasant, in which case, I will eat a cookie!" —*Unknown*.

CHOCOLATE CAKE

They say chocolate is the taste of love. That's probably why it is one of the best comfort foods around. So when you want to treat yourself or a loved one, why not try this easy and tasty chocolate cake recipe? This is one of the easiest, yet tastiest, recipes you'll ever make. Who doesn't like chocolate and simple?

FOR THE CAKE:

3 cups (375 g) all-purpose flour

1½ cups (300 g) granulated sugar

¼ cup (21 g) cocoa powder

2 teaspoons baking soda

1 teaspoon baking powder

1 teaspoon salt

1½ cups (375 ml) plant milk

1 cup (250 ml) vegetable oil

¼ cup (60 ml) white vinegar

FOR THE FROSTING:

2 tablespoons melted coconut oil

½ teaspoon vanilla extract

2 cups (240 g) powdered sugar, plus more as needed

¼ cup (21 g) cocoa powder

¼ cup (60 ml) plant milk

¼ cup (36 g) crushed cashews

FOR THE CAKE:

1. Preheat the oven to 350°F (175°C).

2. Grease an 8-inch (20 cm) round cake pan with a removable bottom. Set aside.

3. In a bowl, whisk together the flour, sugar, cocoa powder, baking soda, baking powder, and salt.

4. Add the plant milk, oil, and vinegar, then beat for 1 minute, until the mixture is smooth. Do not overmix.

5. Pour the batter into the prepared pan and bake for 30 to 45 minutes, or until a toothpick inserted in the center of the cake comes out clean.

6. Let the cake cool for 15 minutes. Remove from the pan, and let cool completely on a wire rack.

FOR THE FROSTING:

7. In a bowl, combine the coconut oil and vanilla. Incorporate the powdered sugar, cocoa powder, and plant milk, one after the other.

8. Beat until the mixture is creamy. (For a stiffer frosting, add more powdered sugar.)

9. Spread the frosting on the cooled cake, then sprinkle with cashews before serving.

SAUCES AND TOPPINGS

MACADAMIA NUT CHEESE

MAKES 3 (1 LB/450 G) VEGAN CHEESES | PREP TIME: 35 MINUTES | COOK TIME: 5 MINUTES |
REST TIME: 15 MINUTES | REFRIGERATION TIME: 2 HOURS

One thing I often hear when people consider becoming vegan is "But I'd never be able to quit eating cheese." Breaking news: you don't have to! This recipe is the perfect base for any vegan cheese. I've included three variants, but the sky's the limit when it comes to flavoring your cheese. So whenever people ask me how I live without cheese, I hand them this recipe.

1. Lightly oil 3 ramekins (½ cup/125 ml each).

2. Pour boiling water over the macadamia nuts and soak for 15 minutes.

3. Drain and transfer the macadamia nuts to a blender.

4. Add the remaining ingredients and blend until smooth.

5. Pour the mixture into a saucepan, then bring to a boil over medium-high heat, stirring constantly. When the mixture reaches the boiling point, keep simmering for 2 minutes, then remove from the heat. If making a variation, add your preferred flavorings (see sidebar). The mixture will be thick and ready to be poured into the ramekins.

6. Pour the mixture into the ramekins. Cover with plastic wrap and refrigerate for at least 2 hours. Enjoy.

¼ cup (36 g) macadamia nuts

1 cup (250 ml) water

⅓ cup (80 ml) solid deodorized coconut oil

¼ cup (15 g) nutritional yeast

2 tablespoons tapioca starch

1 tablespoon powdered agar-agar

1 teaspoon lemon juice

1 teaspoon cider vinegar

1 teaspoon maple syrup

1 teaspoon salt

½ teaspoon garlic powder

VARIATIONS:

To make any of these vegan cheeses, just stir in your preferred flavoring at the end of the cooking process.

BLACK PEPPER VEGAN CHEESE:
Basic recipe plus 1 tablespoon crushed black peppercorns

TRUFFLED VEGAN CHEESE:
Basic recipe plus 1 tablespoon truffle oil

CHILI VEGAN CHEESE:
Basic recipe plus 1 tablespoon chopped canned jalapeño peppers

Tip: Vegan cheese will keep refrigerated for up to 1 week.

PLANT MAYONNAISE

MAKES ABOUT ¾ CUP (180 ML) | PREP TIME: 10 MINUTES

To celebrate my dad's 75th birthday, we took him out to a wonderful vegan restaurant. While I was chatting with family and friends, one of the staff members came by, leaned in, and said, "We are using your vegan mayonnaise recipe!" Now you can bring this easy recipe into your own kitchen.

¼ cup (60 ml) plant milk

1 teaspoon Dijon mustard

1 teaspoon maple syrup

¼ teaspoon salt

½ cup (125 ml) vegetable oil

1 teaspoon lemon juice

1 teaspoon cider vinegar

1. In a blender-proof container, place the plant milk, Dijon mustard, maple syrup, and salt.

2. Blending continuously using a hand blender, drizzle in the oil until the mayonnaise emulsifies.

3. As soon as the mayonnaise starts to thicken, add the lemon juice and cider vinegar. Pulse to combine.

Tip: The plant mayonnaise will keep refrigerated for up to 5 days.

CASHEW PARMESAN

MAKES ABOUT ⅔ CUP (80 G) | PREP TIME: 5 MINUTES

Cashews are so versatile; they make for a perfect substitute for many dairy ingredients, like in this cheese. It's so tasty, fans of Italian food will just love it!

1 clove garlic, minced

⅓ cup (45 g) cashews

⅓ cup (20 g) nutritional yeast

½ teaspoon fleur de sel

1. Place all the ingredients in the bowl of a food processor, then pulse to coarsely chop and combine.

Tip: The cashew parmesan will keep refrigerated for up to 4 days.

MARINATED RED ONIONS

MAKES ABOUT 1 CUP (150 G) | **PREP TIME: 5 MINUTES** | **COOK TIME: 1 TO 2 MINUTES**

I invented this on the fly when I wanted to garnish a dish with a pickled topping. It's so simple and good, and it goes nicely with so many dishes, like my Tacos (page 123).

1. In a small saucepan, combine the vinegar, water, sugar, and salt. Bring to a boil, then add the onion slices. Boil for 1 to 2 minutes.

2. Remove from the heat and set aside.

3. Remove any excess brine from the onions before using by patting them dry with a paper towel.

½ cup (125 ml) white vinegar

½ cup (125 ml) water

2 tablespoons cane sugar or granulated sugar

Pinch of salt

1 red onion, thinly sliced

Tip: The marinated red onions will keep refrigerated in the brine for up to 1 week.

VEGGIE BALLS

MAKES 20 BALLS | PREP TIME: 30 MINUTES | COOK TIME: 25 MINUTES

Sometimes you just want to serve something simple and healthy that the whole family will love. These balls go very well with salad, you can serve them with tomato sauce, or they can even be eaten as a cold snack. I love having these on hand for days when I don't know what to eat and don't feel like cooking. I don't need anything more than a nice soup, my Hummus (page 150), and these veggie balls to be happy.

FOR THE VEGGIE BALLS:

3 cups (90 g) baby spinach

1 (19 oz/540 ml) can chickpeas, rinsed and drained

1 cup (165 g) frozen corn kernels

1 cup (160 g) frozen peas

1 cup (90 g) quick oats

1 cup (108 g) breadcrumbs

¼ cup (15 g) nutritional yeast

1 teaspoon onion powder

1 teaspoon dried oregano

1 teaspoon dried basil

1 teaspoon salt

1 cup (250 ml) plant milk, plus more as needed

Vegetable oil

FOR THE CURRY MAYONNAISE:

½ cup (125 ml) Plant Mayonnaise (page 184)

1 teaspoon curry powder

1 teaspoon maple syrup

Pinch of salt

FOR THE VEGGIE BALLS:

1. Preheat the oven to 375°F (190°C).

2. Add all the ingredients except the plant milk and oil to the bowl of a food processor.

3. With the motor running, slowly add the plant milk. Continue to add milk as necessary until a ball is formed. It shouldn't be too wet.

4. Generously oil a baking sheet. Use an ice-cream scoop to portion the mixture into balls, placing them on the prepared baking sheet as you go.

5. Bake for 15 minutes, flip, and keep baking for 10 minutes more.

FOR THE CURRY MAYONNAISE:

6. Place all the ingredients in a bowl and mix until combined.

7. Drizzle over the veggie balls or place in a separate bowl for dipping.

Tip: You can also deep-fry the veggie balls. The result is less healthy, but so delicious!

TOFU PEPPERONI

MAKES ABOUT 7 OUNCES (200 G) | **PREP TIME: 15 MINUTES** |
COOK TIME: 10 TO 15 MINUTES | **REST TIME: 15 MINUTES**

This tofu pepperoni perfectly captures the pepperoni seasoning and is a perfect topping for your pizza, sandwiches, and crackers.

1. Preheat the oven to 400°F (200°C).

2. Thinly slice the tofu. Using a round cookie cutter, cut out rounds of tofu to simulate the look of pepperoni.

3. In a bowl, combine the nutritional yeast, fennel seeds, oregano, salt, and red pepper flakes.

4. Add the tofu slices and gently turn to coat with the seasonings. Let the tofu rest for 15 minutes to several hours.

5. Generously oil a baking sheet and spread the tofu slices on the sheet.

6. Bake for 10 to 15 minutes.

6 ounces (170 g) extra-firm tofu

2 tablespoons nutritional yeast

½ teaspoon fennel seeds

½ teaspoon dried oregano

½ teaspoon salt

¼ teaspoon red pepper flakes

3 tablespoons vegetable oil or olive oil

Tip: The tofu pepperoni will keep refrigerated for up to 5 days.

SEITAN

SERVES 6 | PREP TIME: 30 MINUTES | COOK TIME: 1 HOUR | REST TIME: 15 MINUTES

Not so long ago, when you heard about vegetarian food, taste wasn't necessarily a top priority. Now, thanks to the growing interest in vegetable protein sources, we have lots of tasty options. Seitan is one of my favorites; it's an excellent substitute for meat in any and all classic dishes. Once it's cooked, it can be grilled, served hot or cold, and used in sandwiches or sauces. It's less fatty than meat or fish, has no cholesterol, and is richer in protein. And above all, it's delicious!

2 cups (260 g) gluten flour, plus more as needed

½ cup (60 g) chickpea flour

½ cup (30 g) nutritional yeast

1 tablespoon smoked paprika

1 tablespoon dried basil

1 tablespoon onion powder

1½ cups (375 ml) hot water

½ cup (125 ml) soy sauce

2 tablespoons vegan Worcestershire sauce

1 tablespoon ketchup

4 cups (1 L) vegetable broth

1. In a large bowl, whisk together the gluten flour, chickpea flour, nutritional yeast, smoked paprika, dried basil, and onion powder.

2. In a second bowl, whisk together the hot water, soy sauce, Worcestershire sauce, and ketchup.

3. Add the wet ingredients to the dry ingredients and stir well.

4. Gather the dough into a ball and knead for 2 to 3 minutes, adding more gluten flour if needed.

5. Tightly wrap the seitan in plastic wrap or in cheesecloth, and tie at both ends.

6. In a large pot, bring the vegetable broth to a boil, then add the seitan. Lower the heat and gently simmer the seitan for 1 hour, flipping it from time to time.

7. Remove the pot from the heat and let the seitan cool in the broth for 15 minutes. Drain the seitan. Unwrap, then serve with bread and your favorite condiments.

Tip: Seitan keeps refrigerated for up to 5 days or frozen for up to 2 months.

DRINKS

COLD-BREWED ICED COFFEE

SERVES 1 | PREP TIME: 5 MINUTES | REFRIGERATION TIME: 2 TO 12 HOURS

I like to start my day with a cup of strong coffee. It helps cure my lack of anxiety. I also love iced coffee, which I firmly believe was created by someone looking for a way to drink even more coffee. But why spend 10 dollars on an iced coffee when you can make it at home? Homemade iced coffee tastes better, contains no chemicals, and has just the amount of sugar you want. With age, I have finally come to understand what my mother meant when she said that homemade is best.

1. In a cup, combine the plant milk, coffee, maple syrup, cocoa powder, and salt.

2. Refrigerate for 2 hours or overnight. The longer the coffee rests, the stronger the taste will be.

3. Strain the mixture and pour over ice.

1½ cups (375 ml) plant milk
2 tablespoons ground coffee
2 tablespoons maple syrup
1 teaspoon cocoa powder
Pinch of salt
Ice cubes, to serve

GOLDEN MILK

One thing I learned to love over the years is yoga—I mean, not to the point of actually practicing it every day, but still. It got me interested in Ayurveda, a form of traditional Indian medicine whose practitioners believe that spices have healing properties. Turmeric is one of the star Ayurveda spices, so here's an energy-boosting sun milk that is the perfect post-yoga drink . . . even if you don't do yoga.

1½ cups (375 ml) plant milk

2 teaspoons maple syrup

1 cinnamon stick

1 star anise

½ teaspoon turmeric

¼ teaspoon ground cardamom

Pinch of salt

1. In a saucepan over medium-high heat, bring all the ingredients to a boil, stirring constantly. Keep a close eye on the saucepan, so the milk doesn't boil over.

2. Remove from the heat and let rest for 10 minutes.

3. Strain the milk and serve.

ORANGE GINGER CHIA FRESCA

MAKES 4 CUPS | PREP TIME: 15 MINUTES

Originally from Central America, chia seeds were the basis of Aztec and Mayan diets. The word "chia" means "strength" in Mayan, likely because chia would fill people with the energy they needed before setting out on long walks. They likely consumed these superseeds not as a porridge, but rather as a drink after soaking them in water and allowing them to expand. Here's one delicious way to enjoy the virtues of this superfood.

4 cups (1 L) orange juice

1 (1-inch/2.5 cm) piece fresh
  ginger, peeled and sliced

¼ cup (40 g) whole chia seeds

Ice cubes, to serve

1. Place all the ingredients except the ice in a blender and process to a smooth consistency.

2. Strain, if desired.

3. Serve over ice.

GINGER LEMONADE

Lemonade or ginger ale? Why do we always need to choose? Why is it so hard to find a lemon-ginger drink out there? I was tired of searching, so I created it. Here's my recipe—go bottle it and get rich!

Juice from 4 lemons

1 (2-inch/5 cm) piece fresh ginger, peeled and coarsely chopped

4 cups (1 L) water

⅓ cup (80 ml) maple syrup

Ice cubes, to serve

2 lemons, sliced, to serve

1. Place the lemon juice and ginger in a blender and process until smooth.

2. Add the water and maple syrup and mix to combine.

3. Strain into a pitcher and then serve over ice, garnished with a slice of lemon.

ACKNOWLEDGMENTS

I want to first thank my wife, Amélie, without whom this project would have never seen the light of day. Her encouragement, support, and more-than-constructive criticism were and will forever be of inestimable value to me. Thanks to Samuel Joubert for his incredible talents as a photographer and jokester. Thanks to Noémie Graugnard for her innate sense of aesthetics and for her kindness. Thanks to Emilie Villeneuve, who was the starting point for this project, for her support. Thanks to Marie Guarnera for her patience. Thanks to Bhavna Chauhan and Robert McCullough for letting me publish this book with such a reputed publishing house as Penguin Random House. Thanks also to Marie Asselin and Katherine Stopa for their exceptional work. Thanks to my mother for instilling in me the pleasure of cooking at an age when I still needed to stand on a chair to reach the counter. Thanks to Natalie Collins for having tested out practically all of my recipes. I'd also like to sincerely thank the thousands of people who follow me on social media, who share my recipes, and who take the time to comment on my posts and write to me in private. Your comments always warm my heart.

INDEX